# Sharing life with love
## By
## Gerry Legister



**ISBN-13:**
**978-1493701483**

**ISBN-10:**
**1493701487**

# Foreword

To coincide with the inspiration of poetry 2011, sharing life with love is a volume of poetry disclosing the heart of our emotions, although some readers may not have the slightest interest in poetry, verses of real life experience dominates the entire book, written from the heart of one of the nation's spiritual aspiring poet.

We will discover that the overall mood of the book is warm and intriguing, furthermore, there are sacred lines woven with beauty with clear rhythm and rhyme that gets hold of the imagination and keeps the mind focus to read all one hundred and ninety poems.

There are plenty of sonnets to give a wishful yearning, and the tapestry of rich spiritual enlightenment to enjoy, there are a few comical ballads to lighten things up with 'Sushi 'and sonnets about breakfast, some are unusually written and crops up unexpectedly.

Sharing life with love seemed reasonably balance and representative selection of the poets best verses, you may be surprise that sharing life with love embraces the popularity of poems accessible online, all the poems are intended to share with the public, and not on the basis solely for poetry lovers. There are some poems that have won writing contest included in this volume, it is a matter of gratitude that they are enlisted, standing out from the obscure and solitary fractions of admiration, the overstretch road full of promises is written with admirable foresight, and the allegory in a thing of fear and boys will be boys suggest the mind of a playful character, but clinical to tempting the lust for life we will cherish the passionate lines of primer gems in a new head of good

In the hand that must be strong
To rule people's hearts far and near,
In native shores of many pilgrim land
The hearts that is willing to hear.

The world pauses now, but later will judge
After the honeymoon stories are written
Of the same speeches on a different page,
And proofs by the world are seen.

# Sharing life with love
## Poetry
### By

# Gerry Legister

# A Jamaican woman

I see a Jamaican woman,
Dancing to reggae music,
She is looking more attractive,
Taken by different shapes of the body,
She moves in a trance to display her beauty,
Ingenuity, paused in aghast breath,
And mystery binds a haven of thought,
To embrace the moment's pleasure,
Winding away in a dark corner,
You can hardly see other dancers near,
Smoking with rhythm inhale,
The addiction of love is sweeter kisses,
Reap silently in the morning coolness.
I see an older Jamaican woman,
Kneeling, praying, digging, and then burying
The sacrifices she understand,
With her love offering in the land,
Society chanting, another reggae song,
This time, guiding the new age mothers,
Weave idle sighs like mourning birds,
Rocking on trees fell by hurricane,
Never had they work in the sugar cane,
And sweetness is a flavour only in the wind,
I see more desirable Jamaican woman,
On exotic parade defining time,
Wearing tiny cloth upon their skin,
I still see them not dancing, but admiring.

# A kiss says it all

We kiss long before we say goodbye,
And you feel lasting passion to thrill,
When there is nothing more to say
Imagination enchantment fills.

Goodbye kisses leaves shadows
Of soft imploding image,
Sauntering along the morrows
With physical camouflage

A kiss prized the heart open
And bring a message through the air,
Arise to haunt everything
Eyes lips and hands share

Engage the waiting atmosphere
Being in love captures desires
The flavour of spring and summer
Gives a heart the greatest pleasures

Although some kisses gently fall,
Not all lips kiss with fire and feelings,
Though they kiss the skin to make a thrill
Indelible moment await the timing.

Kiss me if you mean to marry, Kiss me now, kiss me quick,
For I need reassuring of my vows, my choice, my dream,
And while this illusion last, no other lover than this fact,
I shall find you, and happily romance in between.
Senses touch the nuzzling bite to invade persuasion,
Loves sweetest emotions finds the willing heart,

To share this wonderful pleasure of earthly passion,
And swap health to reign in the crush of parade impart.

The power of the body, comes in language of friendship,
With signals of love, daring to win secrets that attracts,
Flirting men and women into deeper relationship,
By unspoken behaviour the seduction stimulates.

A kiss says it all, inseparable picturesque perfection,
The chiming clock in the mind, finds the sequence,
To fantasy and truth, and right from emotions to affection,
The attraction is different from a brush with chance.

# A Life worth Living

Sweat dripping down into a lingering forge line
To wrinkled brow nested firm on the fretted face,
Through the deep fog into the dark murky mind,
Feeling an aching pain the heart must embrace.

The sharp pain cuts a deep path into the cleft
That's a wound so far it cannot quickly be healed,
From the sudden pain that left the soul bereft
Down in despair creaky bones becomes dried.

The skeleton man works hard for a life worth living,
Paying back the debt the mind owes to society
He looks so weak and frail when the day is ending,
His time is limited but he dares to claim the victory.

In dreams he hears hopes blowing in the breeze,
Softly whisper between the walls and the pencil trees,
The burden carry release began to move with ease,
His awaken soul tumbles upon the wounded knees.

A stream in the soul flows and grows into rivers of cure
Release the struggle to find that life is worth living,
And sense the purposes of reasons we are sent here
Distinction is worth values to prolong the ending.

And finding faith brings joy afresh into his only being,
Blowing opportunities from where he last had seen
His esteem dreams were broken down and left in ruin,

The surge now is to fight for something worth having.

The good of hope and faith in mankind can also be hidden,
When life is lost in the realm that appears to be sacred,
Belief finds providence the reverberated truth within?
By the light making life worth living in all that was dead.

# A New Age

Beyond this present strand,
Herald the dawn of a new age,
With another incomplete generation,
And we leave the past to go on pilgrimage.

People reaching out for a new start,
Fleeing the present awful destiny,
With the shame and guilt of our past,
Crossing the rippling tides of history.

To explore a beautiful concept,
Leaving the dark dusty spirit,
Of this fading world dying debt,
With guilty pleasures we must neglect.

There is doubt in every candidates vote,
Stumbling on with promise accountability,
History rewritten on a new bank note,
And each decision causes more anxiety.

The new age owes no maintenance,
Over the darkness of this generation,
But offers hope and a life more intense,
Than the existence of present cohesion.

I will watch as new horizon turn the page,
Bands play music for the decade to dance,
We wait patiently at the crossing of a new age,
The decision of faith spun by chance.

New age may bring hope and credibility

But only where things exist of simplest nature,
To brighten the future with our destiny,
In pursuit of many more hopeful desire

## **A New Head of Good**

A new spiritual head of good,
In canvas clothes the royalty clad
Among principalities divinely stood
Wave of power in the wand he had.

In the hand that must be strong
To rule people's hearts far and near,
In native shores of many pilgrim land
The hearts that is willing to hear.

The bells chimes make us glad
For we see changes in the wind,
Bring a new vision heading for good,
Avert the dangers and start again.

With this new spiritual head of good
Carry the oracles with humility and care,
Upon the pinnacle of society stood
Advertise self in start of penitent prayer.

The world pauses now, but later will judge
After the honeymoon stories are written
Of the same speeches on a different page,
And proofs by the world are seen.

# A Road Full of Promises

By the time I found out we were already,
Too late to change on the road full of promises,
Hard to let go of things we love and things we try,
Clutch the shadows in sunset of joy and crisis.

Darkness flood the light from dawn converged,
Trying to hold onto everything we deserve,
Changes came to our lives, and crosswords emerged,
Fell in pieces and broken dreams stayed reserve.

No likely end could opportunity bring than sorrow,
And with the cross down drop upon our knees,
The joy was dim and breathes grimacing as we go,
In pulse beat emotions on the road full of promises.

Sweat reared as water ski, coil and swiftly swan,
In the spring of love anxiety ambush the heart,
And tears rang; became dreams come and gone,
In the laden flame that glows fainter by sight.

We meet our fate on the road full of promises,
And in pain, somewhere along the road we stop,
Only to think briefly by guilt fury our gain and loses,
Those that we hate they could have been loved.

The impulse drove windy tumults in our mind,
Search happier state of this life where we had been,
The breath we wasted on the path left behind,
Brought sorrows to define the duty held in a dream.

Some dreams came true from the start to the end,
But the pledge of other promises left unfulfilled,
The reduction were never woken, and went unbroken,
Fortunately they made me smile still in silence stayed.

## A Sacred Gathering

Shadows swamp the air with a blanket of fog,
Move mythical clouds from under the dark sky,
Fitting the past sleekly within our memory,
Familiar faces buried long ago in the cemetery.

Nimbly stood stones erect as ruin pillar post,
Forgotten names shimmer in glory halls of fame,
A sacred gathering in the future with the past,
Meet history looking for friends to rise again.

Spirits gather quietly to watch at every funeral,
A world created to celebrated charm and wit,
Innumerable company posses the ethereal,
Our heroes walk slowly up into hollowed light.

The rapture of delta forces multiply in the sky,
The just are blessed, resurrected and translated,
Churned by the world martyrs greeted in eternity,
And given the rewards joyfully anticipated.

The tears we shed can make our hearts frail,
But in heaven; there will be a sacred gathering,
That no dusty method of frail flesh can assail,
Till all humanity groan in woes be forgiven.

# A Shoulder to Cry Upon

Always ready to listen, without making judgment,
You have been supportive when I am feeling alone.
Whenever I call, you're available when I am in need;
You become the shoulder I can lean upon for help.
And a place of comfort to weep and say how I feel,
When the sun goes down on your perfume face,
Disappointment drilled into the today's confession
I see the future has much to do with our conversation.
And often when I am too weak, I fall asleep too;
Rumours are everywhere that you can't let me go.
Maybe someday, people will see the true picture,
And find out later that they've made a big mistake.
If you tell me to leave I will feel totally crush,
Those moments of uncertainty hurt me as much.
Tomorrow I will come back looking for you
To celebrate the way you made things look new.
You have a right to keep me away locked outside
Many will not see what it's like to be with you inside,
There's nothing wrong with discretion, if we stay,
With each other in love for many more days.
The next time I wake up and feel lonely without you,
I will write a letter and keep it by the bedsit table.
To remind me of the support you always make available,
Until you fall upon my shoulders and I read them to you

# A soft spring rain

From the lower clouds gently falls
A soft spring rain rejuvenating the air,
Descend from the sky small miracle
That we believed renew the atmosphere.

Soft spring rain with sweeping shadows
Sprinkle life upon leaves of the trees,
Meanders down into lanes and meadows,
Hope comes sprightly between showers.

Gives birth to beauty when it starts raining,
We stop to hear the beat tiny drops make.
Soft storm captured in landscapes painting,
All the peaceful sounds an artist can create.

A fine drizzle parting the hard winter rain
Soft mist swirling into enchanted dance,
The scent of wet earth changing the terrain,
Only a gifted eye can see the paved surface.

Emanating with droplets of glistened tapestry,
A soft rain caressing the wind in dark places,
Streaming the kind of invincibility from history,
Weave its way through the window of the eyes.

Tapping waterfalls descend upon absorb roof
And continued beyond the drenched jewels,
Where the rain cool earth we may find the proof
Perfectly finish art before summer kiss the skies

# A Thing of Beauty

A thing of beauty fails in the subdue light,
And before revelation sorrow takes the place
Of the breath of life, with seasons changing swift,
We follow the flight from beginning to the end.
And find again the heart of another brighter summer,
Display a thing of beauty hanging in heaven,
The excitement outstretch with blessings.

In Yorkshire, time moves more slowly by great force,
Than the gales that blow in the busy cities of London,
Searching the shops for things to make people happy,
Time and chance opportunity stirs hostility everywhere,
Within the soul comes murmuring from every town,
Requiring the gold we earn by pleasure spurned.

They lift their voices for heroes and fans to loudly cheer.
The youths loitering till late on darker streets,
The silence of paradise is broken dead leaves falling.
Rustle within the vale, the sound of a strange heroic tale,
Hostility gives chase and trouble engages lawless men.
The spectra of dominance cramp in narrow streets
Police and thieves behind shields make their den,
That midnight mealy flowed between anger and frustration
No good voice was there to stop the banging drum.
Sorrow beat the heart deep sound as a nightmare,
In an awful dream, baffled beleaguered government,
Watch in disbelief hostility played out on the streets,
While they clasp their hands and wait for the mist to lift,
Youths with hooded tops, caps and trainers go on the run.
Planned discreet games and making mocking noises,
When the cathedral bell toll it will tell the awful story

That society has failed; if this is the only heritage.
Then the shuffling future looks bleaker and further away,
Than the unemployed on the streets where I live,
Proclaiming morning, evening and night time prayers,
The ghostly host of spirit breaks far into the air,
With a rushing wave like a trouble army on sentry pace,
Even the solemn church bells could not stop,
Phantom cars driving along over hump back roads.
Yorkshire was a thing of beauty, picturesque
History making the benign heritage we have.

Policemen stop the youths and question them,
I am kin to the dilemma that is taking place,
And here I pine between these narrow streets,
Wishing for a better life than the one I behold.
History in making will tell a different story,
From a hidden agenda truth will not be known,
Most will believe a lie, and practice deception.
What a tribulation, chaos and confusion.

And Yorkshire smoke will hide all the fears,
We only the faint glimpses of future years,
And sad tears began dripping from mine eyes,
Into a silent prayer for the children of tomorrow,
And Heaven knows the pain of my heart,
Yorkshire too will bath in the blood of sorrow.

But in picturesque villages are some good things,
That lies unseen below the clouds and the skies,
Where free bird soars as angels spread their wings
A thing of beauty glow in the sun, moon, and stars.
A blanket to cover the saints from evil all devices,
And protect them from the snare of the fowler
And noisome pestilence that walks at noonday.

God looks out at the night upon the houses,
From out of the heavenly skies, he can see in the dark,
Hear our speech, see our tears, and know our years.
When the dew is dried and morning rain seemed stark

I know the way to mount Zion, after church of God,
And Wesleyans looking back at what they had,
Long ago left on the sidewalk where dogs walk,
Narrow minds looking for joy than cannot be found,
Puzzle by the strangest art sometimes they bark,
Unnecessarily at people they don't like meddling.
On path the police find emptiness driving around,
In cosy cars breaking traffic lights on radon call,

Hour by hour the tribulation trauma starts to creeps in
Upon the Yorkshire moors finding more squally rain
And the peace we have dream about in the countryside
Can be found in the cities of Leeds and York,

Save in the splendour of our dreams, when the wit is in
The pleasure of intoxication creeps slowly out
And we behold the ramifications not in its full glory
For in time of recovery desire surely will come again
Unto young men and women looking like half dress fairy
Slowly sinking into a dismal realm.

Behind the hills; with the smoke going higher into the air
And the dead depart to heaven go above the white trees
Glimmering in the starlight: they join other waiting ghosts
From life they had been we will know them no more.

Sometimes the cold wind that rises in the dead of night
Suddenly sweeps inward from scarbough to York
Rustling the heather on Likely moors with a weeping voice
Whistling through the blackness with mournful wail,

Echoing at evening from the Yorkshire foot hills.
In many joyless homes relationships are broken,
Children home alone, left with dogs and cuddling cats
Seek comfort when fathers are absent or drop in unseen.

In Yorkshire life was honey sweet burst into bloom
We hear the sweetest tune played in the stillness at even
And the melody goes out with the shadows at night
Surrounded by hopeful anticipation of divine favour
The stars covet our lowly existence and soon the towns,
Burst with riotous living even the corners of quiet valleys,
Are not spared the trauma fast fall the troublesome seal,

And many voices lament for these things to go away.
From that love country all that has been violate,
A thing of beauty I found in churches where I pray

Happy days have seen the lamp burns with bright glow.
Yorkshire was the valley of my paradise, unstrained delight,
By the familiar path I have walked, to find again my dream?
In the garden of lilies' and roses formed bright,
In Yorkshire once before, I met some heavenly friends,
And society had stolen a part of my heart,
I only hear their names now and again.

# A Thing of Fear

When Spiders camouflage they can eat
In places where they don't belong
Their silence propose a web of deceit
Beautiful thing arthropods air breathing.

Their maligned reputation identify fear
Buzzing in caves and combing the ground
Discrete creeper expert timing in magic lair,
Weave up and down realm without a sound.

Feared by most crawlies climbing up the wall
Being small unfairly treated by humans
The leathery covering distinguish them all
Nature adorns their elongated forms.

Before the day passes away too quickly
The philandering spider sees the bright world,
And want to reach the sky with the butterfly
Light the leathery lawn before night grows cold.

A dark thing of our fear we cannot ignore
They live in palaces mostly alone,
Look for them on streets corners and in the air
Weaving their cobwebs in homes made of stone.

# A time is coming

The bruises you have gained may have caused you pain
The hurt you are feeling inside will find healing in time,
When the heart from demise climb safely to sublime aim,
Reach higher into a frame for greater purpose of mind.

A time is coming to leave the changes of things behind,
Those others may follow footprints defining success in life,
Journeying with pain to share enchantment sometime,
Unfriendly terrain helps delay the ending of bitter grief.

Good friends when free can help to mend the broken way,
Although they care; may not stay to play or share a taunt,
To the awakened mind crept back into decline each day,
And wash the stain of hope with the tears they supplant.

Time is the kindest healing merchant you will ever find
Takes the longest way to come comfort the broken heart,
Surround all the loses when cost betrayed searching mind,
Whether in pride or Art the timing can make a new start.

The best power of healing time coming takes a little while,
It stops and starts to fix the barrier rife of human feelings,
Sunk deep in disillusion state our vast seclusion's are real,
When truth stands alone quietness of sweetness it brings.

Tasting together the bitter desire in charms that merit growth,
Lasting shoots culminating in dept and inner harmony,
Healing has given a new life to the place we go upon earth,
Treasured memories saunter in the moments of victory.

# **The Abused**

Words go tearing deep to hide you
Locked away into a horrible prison,
Making you feel in a state of lesser value,
And wish to change and be another person.

The abuse that you hate most can hurt,
Birth tears which becomes a river of fire,
To burn with anger how you have felt,
And gently draw your soul into fear.

The abused in rooms sharing swollen faces
The vivid blur make tables and chair shake,
Keen to hide all the anxiety emotion traces,
Seek revenge for any convictions make.

But pride holds you a nobler prisoner in chains,
Ransom your emotions breaking out into pity,
Towards them who are controlling the pains
The intensity makes you feel life is empty.

The darkness of the night is full of intense,
Raging war of words colour the extreme sounds,
Severely evoke tense and feeble defence,
The unpleasant degree of coldness groans.

From depths, profound raging goes unabated,
Crying out seemingly to forgive deeds done,
By the violent, wild and often aggravated,
You will discover more marks that are not shown.

Around your dreams is a great freedom girdle,
A tide to wipe inclined tears when you lament,

About the insane drive reacts to jump each hurdle,
Inspire hope to escape the cruel torment.

But the road ahead moves slowly downwards,
Out of range the pain is temporally broken,
All the abusive memories will turn towards
The new door you are looking to open.


## **Accomplish my desire**


Day will be darkness and not light,
It will be as though rattled birthright fled,
In waterfall woeful darkness greet,
The persecuted day that was once good.

Desire leaned away on a stubborn wall,
Waiting with no brightness in it,
For a serpent had bitten the night fall,
As though trip by a hurricane poet.

Life blows higher accomplish my desire,
House in a mole, when my soul is in mourning,
And my heart turns and burns like fire,
In waking haste refuse sleep restlessly drifting.

Climbs back to bed and more troubles find,
Desires every time tumbling black and white,
Dreams swamp the decks of my mind,
Tormenting daily trials every moment conceit.

Where desire comes in a tunnel of gutter,
As tempest storm stain the crinkled nightgown,
And dreaming deep fall blind into heavenly fire,
Mocking thoughts comes to a bad end.

# Afraid to love

When love was sweet and life was good,
I thought I could never love anyone as deep,
Optimism found me in another mood,
And made promise to live and die to keep.

But after I found out the painful truth,
My heart rearranges and preserves the pain,
Hold each moment within a single thought,
I became afraid to love again.

And all the promises kind winds blow,
Opportunity into lovely notes of pleasant tune,
Through the door and at my window,
I am still afraid to love again.

When I fall asleep capsize into twisted realism,
In tears I tell myself the only secret I fear,
If chance comes by I may never love again,
Although I long to share the joy with another.

Who may be standing somewhere in the shadow,
And stare at me, but I am bound to be there,
I've turn away, yet if love could make the fear go,
And become the vestige of care.

What love so great can set my spirit free?
By night and day freedom gain from fear,
Left deep compositions haunting me,
In moods and wounds which go deep and near.

# After church

We collect the hymn books passing through the pew,
And look good, with grace to look for a little while,
Then we decide it's time to leave the chosen few,
And take the journey for a mile with faded smile.

After church service benediction at last spring,
The welcome presence of another serenity fall,
We quickly part in heart from the praises we sing,
On roads converged, hardly a note we can recall.

We feel the food destined to eat, and the warm,
Taste climbs up for a pleasing trip into our lips,
Down the lane, leaving church feeding the brain,
With aromas tricks, temptation tried with many slips.

After church we forget home is another branch,
Lost in jest, caught in play, unseen eyes watching,
The rest of the day, and the eyes continue to watch,
Through the night and haunt the mind until morning.

# Aging

I didn't think about aging while rushing around,
Getting old unlearned, I thought as a veteran,
I am strong enough to run round the world,
Come back, and start again at night and at dawn.

But orchard youth had decoy the hoary glow,
For superior strength was needed for courage,
To do much more then; than what I can do now,
Exploits adorned with dreams and weakling age.

Getting near the fire and implacable ash ground,
The hollow rites prepared and already forgotten,
The soul in wrinkled body I carry myself around,
Do not see the shame of the age I own.

Were we too old; when we started getting mad?
For age passes through every cycle of our life,
And decide timely experience for what we had,
Giving strength enough to climb, and leave and seek.

In all pursuit, we decide when heart has no desire,
To go on as long as we live and let age determine,
When there's no more passion to extinguish the fire,
That has the flames going higher into heaven.

# <u>Agony</u>

Tempted and tried we often wander,
How life has given us agonizing pains,
Raging war on every unconquered shore,
Unquenched flame burning a fire within,

Agony light up the soul with a bewildered glow,
Tattered lives mirror the inevitable existence,
Of hopeless demise into confuse sorrow,
Pushing emotions to the edge of tolerance.

Through sapping energy the sweat descend,
Purge the heart consume with agonized flames,
Separating the language of friends,
With blistering tragedy hope begins.

Detoxify poison in the body driven to the core,
People try every way to avoid temptation,
Suffocating beneath the consequences implore,
The conscience is a lively fire within.

Bunning flames take earth out of control,
Every person's future is in purgatory,
Spirits fight to capture the tormented soul,
Walking the timeless realms into eternity.

The rhapsody of agony encamp in the heart
The light of happiness waiting at the door
To unveil the anguish truth will impart
With many more choices to discover

# **Angel far away**

You're my angel far away in another land
Reflections of you come in words of a song
Emotions cry day and night to hold your hand
And the silent dream lives on to become strong.

You are an angel of love sent into my dream,
Enthuse my being with fire aflame in my soul
Make me clean wash by the eternal stream
And hide me within from the stains of world.

For the gold you're holding can make me whole
Take me to your throne to find that illusive crown,
Ambition driven wild by the pursuit in my soul
Flown on clouds to another town may call my own.

Far away from this terrain where you too are alone
To embrace the bliss we have tasted in my dream
And see the stars pointing the way to a new home
Gather the rewards to build a bridge of stone.

Sown like seeds in the land by faith we perceived
Summer flakes where sunny crystals gates gleam,
Brighter images esteemed the open mind conceived
The glow of your halo reflects in the eternal stream.

# **<u>Angels</u>**

In ever increasing blessings of ceaseless flow,
Running over with ten thousand ageless beings
Pass from earth daily carriage to and fro.
Keepers of mortal souls in heaven are unseen,

In halo vestment robe in paradise glorious light
Their good and great deeds we have esteem
Gospel champions by appointment for the right
Reasons protect choices made in every season.

Fairy angels alluring appears in many dreams
Share the message and leaves the limelight
To expose the chronicles of ceaseless humans
Express the thrill and pain of transforming sight.

In the ever expanse of heaven celestial glow
Angels passing from earth to different globe
All the terrestrial mysteries we may never know
Nor understand the symbols worn on their robe.

But a charge to keep mortal souls in heavens view
Ministries renew the fervour of ageless conquest
Given by supreme force the course of destiny review
Old and new will share their fate at the final inquest.

# <u>Angels on Butterfly Wings</u>

Some thought they met God, and good relations
But divine paradise requires greater expectation,
Than the zeal men preach when they have an itch,
They travel a road not paved with good intentions,
Find fault with everyone holding different views.
Vows of circumcisions make thoughtful decisions,
In the heart there is a beautiful serene park.
A safe retreat where God can come and walk,
Visions can lift our heads high into the clouds,
To watch angels on butterfly wings come down.
From land beyond view under waterfall skies,
We see them make friends in our cottage homes.
Moving around silently as butterflies awkwardly do,
Falling stars guiding society into more changes,
Crystallite each day into something new,
They open the windows that transport our fortune.
And slippery faults are embedded in our way,
We try to live a good life, believe God and Jesus.
Look for answers to the prayers we pray.
It seems like a long journey, but it is really short.
And God watches us from heaven every day,
See how we play make games and have fun
While we grow old waiting for love and dreams,
Wait patiently until the moment has come.

# At the end of the night

At the ending of the night, memory not as bright,
As fowls eyes shine upon branches in the dark
Our nature they stark, dare to claim a better sight,
Over those wanton bars filled with spirit talk.

And broken vows our conscience fled and dread,
Lay siege in our head, the tide of graves dreams,
Try to force our stumbling way to another's bed
At the end of night with short lived passions.

We know the finale when everything seems fine,
And people in droves quickly fade from the street,
We change direction and listen to another tune,
Now is a good time to say goodnight.

We'll sleep thorough nightmares, lose sight of time
And become reclined in dreams of sublime pleasure
Wake at interval to see if the weather is fine,
Go back to sleep dare to dream for another hour.

The journey feels good, making up for yesterday,
When the day was grey and the evening stayed
Waiting for the silhouette to pass over the valley,
Come under the canopy of darkness that was made.

By the end of night, fortunate ones take a journey
Far into the labyrinth of spiritual awakening,
And are shown the gates of nights darkest mystery,
Before the dawn slip away into a new beginning.

# Beyond Gender

Design by a senses of fathomless euphoria,
Surpass by Gods unrelenting glory,
This divine power makes the world unique,
For us to argue, disagree and enjoy.

We have attributes inspired by creative order,
Beyond gender in configuration of divine art,
Comes the extraordinary senses propel together,
The perfect way to make a new generation start.

God is neither angel, nor man, nor mechanical,
The emblem he uses defines our identity,
Ebullient creator of male and female,
Author of mystique untamed entity.

Timeless metamorphous intricately refined,
Attracted to masculine and femininity,
We are the profitable increment of mankind,
Exercising divine power with infinity.

Beyond gender we squander when they can,
Our feelings in passions and mischief,
Driving the soul to find eternal demand,
In wisdom beyond the pleasure we achieve.

Bordering with the unequal endowment,
Time connect a new power to advance,
Perform creation with the seduction again,
Opportunity given with s a second chance.

Unleashing euphemism beyond gender,
Distinguish characteristic support,
Alleviating pain for spouse or lover,
We see our calling only as entities of divine faith.

# Birds in the Air

The orchard birds are singing
Peeping over the rosebushes
From greening trees in Silver Spring
Blend in the wind their torrent voices.

Under their hoods of adorable feathers
Warm tiny bodies began twitching
Upon twigs where sunlight strives,
Hide upon shoots in timid pose waiting.

When sunshine smiles upon them
Birds of same feathers stay together
Flying over hills, blossom lawns paved green,
Together they form a line in the air.

Exhibit thrills express in the way they live
Birds gliding abound on torrent heap,
Spreading wings in dazzling dive
Through the clouds they sweep.

Birds in the air don't have our confusion
Make a sound, run mad and cause a riot,
When they are rehearsing flight formation
They can hear us laugh but they are quiet.

# Innocent Birth

From the cradle of innocent birth,
Comes the embracing touch of immaculate worth,
Amidst sweeping streams of watery weariness,
Looming life awakening tender delicate features,
Beauty only a breath away from facing a new world,
The end event begins reality; strong and sacred,
Bright and sanguine, first they are soft then toned,
And every celebration honours the new home.
Drawn by skilful proportion through wavering pool,
From cradled rest to wanton breast of a mother's womb,
Where the realm of nature gives birth to life,
And creation groan with stronger breathe incite,
Birth let time bring delivery of beautiful species,
Which knows not the wait the universe accepts?

# Black Ash

Up Into the sky the smoke blast,
And black ash covered white clouds,
Overseas and streams aghast,
With lashing dust and darken moods.

Slowly passing over earth and ocean,
Disturb the leaves in the noon day,
And halt the easy flights of locomotion,
Painting the ecliptic sky black and grey

Guide the shifting floating vapour,
In serene dominion without a compass,
Wind and time create the power,
And find the path over winding paradise.

Black ash spread in dept too dark to see,
Dissolving material in swaying motion,
Ignorant of pain erupting like infinity,
And flow over the entire beautiful heaven.

Black ash shedding tear and terror,
In the arms of a wicked volcano blast,
The world stood tripping with fear,
Hear the thunder and lightning flash.

New signs in blood vapour and smoke,
A living force with cape and wings,
Breaking chains through space invoke,
Climate change burning things.

Travellers groan, in struggles and fits,

Black ash loiter in places where worlds surrender,
Bemused mankind left with many stitches,
To build a better memorial in the atmosphere.

# Borrowed Places

I hear the rustling of leaves in the trees,
The wind moves and changes direction with ease.
Blow new seasons to earth from the sky,
And open heavens window for a day.
We shower with the dew of early clouds,
Sunrise unfolds and galaxies declines in moods,
We are cocoon in thoughts of our own,
Images of places borrowed, becomes our home.
Traces of memories, making regular rounds,
Some pass by in mute shadows, others in the clouds,
We see them half turn going into the distance,
Life for brief moments is carried in a trance.
They surface and dance in familiar circles,
We see faces, and take pictures in borrowed places,
We the society of mankind, will go to join them,
Our troubles and trials on earth will soon be done.
We are only hired vessels on borrowed time,
Acting as geniuses, with tools in labyrinth of the sublime.
We take our chances whenever we find opportunity,
To challenge the ways we go to our destiny.

# <u>Boys will be boys</u>

In dominion where sadness looms steps had the gloom
Determine to let boys make their own edgy mistakes,
Unafraid, they find courage again to embrace dream,
And doom becomes the light springs when morning rises.

And drift into another day when red eyes went astray,
Burning lust and dust down the vague road to another
Starlit games find chances to reactivate venue and play
But fortunes favour the boys who stop to ponder.

Sometimes they talk and don't turn up to do anything,
When you need them most they leave things to burn,
Iron and pottery, ruffle and tussle waging war waiting
To heap on friends fire of forgiveness in the engine room.

There is a body of opinion, mythical and delusional,
Boys will be boys embark on missions together
Scroungers, soldier's follow after fellow professional,
Wind and rain cannot nullify any of their splendour.

Loved by girls in the wildest arena passions evoke,
Income years turn the journey from boys into men,
No more toys to change and make them fit for work
Only older veterans dream of honour and illusions.

# **Breathlessness**

Every second minute of the day
Excitement entices the eternal passions,
It is the desire to mate and burn away,
The night in uncanny positions.

Breathlessness erupts like volcanoes,
And when it subsides in satisfaction
You are caught in a net with many holes,
Which leaves the mind to make a decision?

Telling you some truth for you to blush,
With what is left from pictures and images,
Entwined together in feelings you'll cherish,
Every sixty minute of the day your body aches.

Dreams lying awake in art and fortitude
Express the sentiments in less dewy eyes terms,
Those happier moments will come to conclude,
There is more to love that fading memories.

When all the pretty words have fallen,
Quicker than you believe love can leave you breathless,
There is something in you stronger than you seem
And smarter than all the empty promises.

That is, if you realize passion is the first stage of desire,
From one who loves the other, even being set apart?
There is something you must always remember,
Love grows stronger in the heart.

# <u>Can you Dance with me?</u>

Can you dance with me if no one else can?
Zumba on the shape that needs some toning
I see myself in the spell of someone's hand
Under their command until I become strong.

In another playlist of my beautiful dream
Perched high dangling on edge in the sky,
Showing the place where I am coming from
I can see gravity fly and my world goes by.

Into sparkling mezzanine on which we dance,
Taking breathtaking leaps and stunning swings,
The intense accentuated a sparkling romance,
Into peaks streaks and cotton wool valleys.

Can you dance with me and get a little closer
Would you like to hold me until we are together?

# <u>Celestial Glow</u>

Dreams came and flooded the room inside,
Took my soul in daring flight to another age,
Leaving the dangers of the world outside
And shadows came near the windows edge.

Falling to the ground without awakening sound
Terrestrial noises no one heard or felt the fear,
Carried in tears by the howling travelling wind,
That was passes in dreams cold and bare.

Standing there wet with dew of the morning air,
And dare not venture to explain the celestial thing,
Of pain already in vein will haunt the atmosphere,
And make memories come more unnerving.

But we see our spirit called into the celestial way,
Not many come as near for the light is bright,
In the heavenly place where we are going one day,
And will see the Lord and all the angels in flight.

Though our sight is poor, we will still see the light,
Circled in rainbow colours high up in celestial glow,
Above the world and the earth beneath our feet,
Break open to kindle the dreams we had long ago.

Ruptured faces and noble figures went unfound,
In haste has fled and sped to finish the better race,
While others were old and still had the good mind
Break to finalize retirement plans in a sunny place.

# Central society

The most amazing thing
Comes from sight and sound
When a child is born again
Into a most unlikely background

And be not influence by bad things
They hear going around every time
Going on in central society,
We find them not too far behind.

Symbolism of the great and the good,
With immediate sense of euphoria,
Find the measures to get ahead
Allow circumstances the lava.

That will dispel doubt and fear
Keep you down with sorrow and grief
And stop you from growing stronger
But keep striving for goals in your life.

# <u>Changing circumstances</u>

Nerves crack and slit,
Changing faces all through the night,
Fluttering with different mast,
Beat the withered veins in either breast,
We curse the crocus day,
Mildew without decent pay,
Changing circumstances,
Lost the opportunities and chances,
Jingle and crushed with cruel blow,
Joy wrench from this present life,
To hear no more prayers,
Nor received fragrances and flowers,
Pleasures swept by in persistent strife,
Into the sunken bubble we drop down,
Upon memory deep churning ocean,
To hear no more the sweetest melody,
Echo when time turn to dash away
From earth we are swallowed by time,
Leaving the thinnest skeleton behind.

# <u>Chase the Devil Away</u>

Chase away the devil
When he comes into your path,
He is just something evil
And you will have the last laugh.

His tricks aren't any surprise
Roaring like a hungry lion
Threatening people's lives
Chase away the devil if you can.

Think of him as proud Satan
Trying to be friend with incantation,
Don't close your eyes to his temptation
See the real picture in regeneration.

Justice is coming and he doesn't expect it,
Because he has crossed the line
He will be bound in the bottomless pit
Put away from society for a long time.

Gods law is strong It will stand when he falls,
Into the prison of his own captivity,
You can say a prayer and close your eyes,
He'll not bother you again throughout eternity.

# Cheating Hearts

Betrayal is more difficult to define,
You can see the trouble it cause,
We may find it even if our manners are fine,
And still not rest until given justice.

Hurt is more inside than the smile wear outside,
External pleasure may give temporary delight,
Torn between what can be and what we hide,
But with the conscience there is a real fight.

Caught within inexpressible blissful plight,
Cheating is not a thing counted in duty,
It matters more to do what is right,
Than to lead a life of excessive vanity.

Chastity is where real happiness lies in purity,
Body and mind may adore pleasures that bring
Mistakes made, but grace is given for sympathy,
And passion from cheating is sorrows awaken.

When the flurries of torment is not forgiven,
In cheating hearts the beauty of perfection is spoil,
The heart long for joy at the same time,
But permanence finds no way to escape the turmoil.

# __Choices__

Will our choices make a difference?
If we live for ourselves or to forgive others,
Though buffeted by agitated wind and tide,
Driven by faith to take responsibility serious,
Is it an earthly calling from higher altitude?
To make the right choice; choosing not to lose
The connecting medium between God and man,
Grant glimpse to see images of the future
If the human spirit is given a second chance,
And face the mirror; can it change the world?
To make us look younger and live a little longer,
Must we celebrate the treasures in a trance?
Surrender to mankind the images in our mind
Or waken gladly to distinguish it from all other.
The glories of heaven conceal hidden cost,
Cast everything below, but hastily look above
The sky is the mirror which holds our future
Being with fortitude hope will never be lost.
Dare to dream by esteeming earthly wisdom,
Knowledge alone was never soul satisfying.
Especially if we find the hidden kingdom,
Whether or not the choices we made were right,
We must accept our mistakes and in passion
Eclipse apocalypse of the daunting Holy Grail.
Another world exist aware of this torment,
And yearn for the former lust as treasures,
For the choices we made guaranteed no bail.
But what we know resembles grand allusions
In messages flash strange images of the future,
Representing the state of the world we are in.
Invite crazed delusions to channel the mind,

Sunk beneath the tempest dangled danger zone,
Prosperity doing harm; charm disloyal crimes,
We try to ride out the storm in confidence.
Breaking promises every time to our children
Had we the right mind we could have won,
When we had lived and everything was fine,
With the weight of sin inevitable grief must come.

# <u>Cold Images</u>

The coin in the mind is very hard to define
The scale of pain passing through the family line
Take the sword and face the challenges of disease
Demons in the soul make our dreams freeze

Make a splash in the fountain of mysteries
The sword I hold unlock the cold images within
The dreams with hope brings greater gains,
More stars I see through the wet stain rain.

Here I see cold images through foggy windows
Wrapped up in time with my bleak surrounding,
That draws the cold breeze and icy winds
So thin the wire cuts through my thinking.

On troubled moors cold images bleached the air
Refresh my wills and drifts away into the atmosphere.

# Communication

This generation found a form of communication,
They want the world to share with technology here,
A language learned they had already forgotten,
All the trails led through year's pioneers uncover.

Where myth goes on the same road the sane went,
In golden verses they swiftly go insanely mad,
And somewhere sad among words the indignant,
Teachers went, torn from symbols where time stood.

In posture of silent expression; transmission invade,
Tiptoeing between hanging sound moving gesture,
To find the myth of communication proverbs made,
Advance in codes, ringing the rich and many poorer.

That unique people on a line swung many times,
All the fiery swords hunts past tense and dance,
In trance, romance inspiring tunes written in songs,
And draw love spellbound into modern sentence.

Earths tribes, with their own languages communicate,
At ease, some on bended knees, even birds in the trees,
Down to bees, and chimpanzees, the mystery create,
A dept of good deeds scurrying pass the years.

Winning, spinning and stroking the tongue of fire,
Nations join together, the smoke blow negotiation,
Higher in familiar tongue, set alight with habitual desire,
And everything is measured through our communication.

## Conquering Passion

Wrestling joy speed to her spirit,
At once dreams dissolved into love,
In the rasping wait at the paradise gate,
Peace comes in dreams that heavenly hopes gave.

Trying to conquer passion inside the mind,
Infatuation of danger which is perfectly unseen,
Across miles excite the sensations we will find,
Engage apprehension with feelings from within.

We do not know the measure of hope giving
Forethought to the consequences we face,
In this craze cause the emotions we are feeling,
Having the outbursts of obsessions we taste.

Individuals conform to the use of good behaviour,
Society will try to conquer the rage of our passion,
But the quest to achieve your love will grow stronger,
We know the qualities of request will take their turn.

Once the fire starts a flame will begin to burn bright,
Strong heat may be difficult to control from a distance,
We will do as well to conquer its powerful might,
On the pathway of dreams we share in a trance.

Life is far too short to leave this love behind,
If it takes one second out of your precious time,
It will affect the emotions and state of mind,
Training our thoughts to leave or become sublime.

# Contemplation

I take this thought into contemplation,
That our days have been a dream,
And in the vision we were the one enthrone,
And no phantom could come between,
Or find the gift to intervene our contemplation.
I only hear the clarity of your voice,
And felt reassurance of peaceful embrace,
Softly echoed in your textured defence,
Like the glorious note in warbling trance,
Contemplating the time we share,
In bond of recurrent years together.
I feel emotions twitch inside and surrendered,
Waltzing in slow steps to a beautiful serenade,
The fulfilment of our visions and dreams,
Bless seasons, wit reasons and happy times,
Speak with tears of delight from your eyes,
With memories looking back over our lives.
When we first met the love we felt,
And tied passion of ribbons around our waist,
With the never ending feeling of you inside,
I contemplate the distraction I wanted to hide,
But when you laugh, everything turns on the magic,
And dispels sadness and anything tragic,
Every time I saw you in the light, and in the night
With invisible strength the future looked bright.
Parting the waves that carried the doubts,
And climb over continents higher than clouds,
And gaze upon the magnificence of lover.
From the ghostly realm hidden above,
Spirit roaring pass and rushing onwards,
Leaving the past behind on dark roads,
I see your image entwined the ripples of my mind.

And I contemplate out of borrowed time,
Until the dream became the magnificence of grace,
Embrace fulfilment in a trance.

# Crumbling Paradise

Our paradise is a beautiful place in mind,
Exist only when we go there in spirit,
On a trip; in this realm of splendid sublime,
Only those so deep in love can get to it.

A precious place of graceful escapades,
Found in the wind that floats through the air,
Dare to be where our daily memory fades,
And fond embrace becomes the treasure.

We seek more from this impure life,
And would endure every pain and torment,
But fiery trials esteem the crumbling grief,
These are the broken promise presently sent.

Burning desire more consuming than fire,
Within me lift the flames to a new heaven,
Overwhelm to speak of any intruder,
Pushing me out and trying to break in.

We fall down but love made us get up again,
With broken dreams of crumbling paradise,
There is no tears heaven; sorrow or pain,
We make our dreams here living in disguise.

No sweet exhale can make this paradise crumble,
Only truth we share divides the beat in our heart,
To make us stop and stare and quietly stumble,
Until we find the truest path where eternity start.

# **<u>Dance Recital</u>**

You may dismiss me during the fast
Moving performances taking place,
Pay more attention to costume and cast
A spell over those sitting in the audience.

If you had sons or daughters in the dance
You would know what this means outside,
Stood behind the crowd to get one chance,
And join forces to cheer the recital inside.

Before the end we congratulate the children,
Because they had done something new
To hear others opinion and had a great time,
Waiting in the auditorium for another review.

The thrill of recitals is filled with pleasure
Around the stage whole families are waiting
Moments to treasure the experience together,
And know recital time is even more amazing.

Voices on screen caught joy in a million pieces,
And there is a finale all entertainers gather in,
A sort of camaraderie hierarchy of artistic faces,
Took their deserved bow for gladly performing.

# Dancing under the Moonlight

Let the stars fly away and leave the moon shining,
With You and I dancing under the light until morning,
Hear the music playing to the tune of your heartbeat
Spiral waltz into the atmosphere in the circle of heat.
Swing under the moonlight and be lost in love's delight,
Souls in unison, while shaking, and twisting in the night,
Fantasy performed in the body moving from side to side,
Magical pleasure the souvenirs reminisce with pride.
Imagine the night where the moon glows in a fountain
The tiniest lives from natures hive paddle in the ripples,
Lift the mind into the songs with picturesque scenes.
And you smile in that moment to cast a wishful token,
With one great look into faith at dreams destiny create,
The amazing aura in which your desire can participate,
Leaving moves in photos to embrace the ambiance found.
Being romantic; the party stood silhouette around,
Shadows swing from the walls unto the dance floor,
You hear the sound but your body cries out for more.
Into the moonlight the eyes are blinded by heavenly bliss,
And the glittering stars appear again in the halo of a kiss.

# <u>Dancing with the stars</u>

Airy tune plays the starry notes we adore
Wind generate the breathe of vibrancy found,
A beat tapping polite crescendo upon the floor,
Judges joined in the finale of encore sound.

Notes spinning in flames swirling the flare around,
The enchantment full of awesome performance,
Shifting body weight perfectly from off the ground,
Contestants wooed the crowd with exotic dance.

Disco costume the glamour of appearance calling,
Showbiz trial before platform of bigger audience,
Dancing with the stars until your eyes are shining,
Don't think you come here to hang out in a trance.

Into this magical movement of swing and speed
Trapped charm glowing in space by metallic plates,
The choreography steps and style will succeed,
To shuffle the dances different combination creates.

We want to have the audience upon their feet,
But we don't know yet; how much we love dancing
Until television shows the moves we often repeat,
Bring out the best twists and turns from within.

Unique blend for either student or entertainment,
Evoke rhythm seductive flames with creative elements,
Flown to where the original inspiration went,
They are allowed to dance with unique movements.

Fluttering like trees continuous wave in the breeze,
When all at once you have the crowd on their knees
Their outstretch hands hope for more to receive,
And you finally become a twinkle in their eyes.

Lively bodies enthused with jiving to the end,
Dancing with stars in modes of thousand sequins,
The choreography disguises shapes with each bend,
You have your hips swaying more tantalizing.

# Darts of intrigue

A shadow from hell in swanky song
Boiling the mind and fiery tongue
With pelting evil the heart has spun
Firing darts of nervy intrigue.

Darts at the heart where love dwells,
The arrow of lives speeds into heaven
But hate is the deep unfathomable wells
Descend into murky drumbeats again.

Humanity wrapped in black shroud
Drama comes with the intrigue of mirth,
But values are forgotten in diminish gold,
Exchange integrity for lesser worth.

We are friends here on the earth,
With weakling hands amides the bliss
Surviving on borrowed time and breath
We exchange fleeting kisses.

Going further back to where the soul reaches,
By creating hands from the ground
Until we are so weak in dangling ditches,
We cannot make a single sound.

# Death at Passover

Life overcomes death,
When Lent of days
Proclaim the power gained.

Over pharaohs land
Already smitten by angelic hand
When death Passover.

Saved by grace
The Hebrew race
Snatched away just in time.

The gathering force
Celebrated and dance
When death Passover

Pharaohs land was empty
Many were smitten by angelic hand
When death Passover.

# <u>Desire</u>

There stood before me is a familiar exploit,
With fantasise in pictures of my desire?
The anxiety of joy running astonishingly hot,
Uncontrollable embers launched into fire.

A flame cascading and advances through the air,
Attack beneath the skin pleasures connecting
My heart permits the trip of a rippling order,
Cross all boarders' adventures exploring.

Leading the way to become the hunted victim,
Euphoria caught in this glorious weakness,
Soul thrown into confusion or desired prison,
Now so close I smell the flavour with each kiss.

The chorus tearing into different parts of my heart,
Bathed now in the agreement of light tranquillity,
The beautiful encounter soaring into the night
Sweetness soaks the air inside warm and lovely.

Dreams among the gentrification of this felicity,
Only reclaimed the amazing droplets of desire,
In daylight find a less infamous route to reality,
To take my soul and filled it with more pleasure.

# Having Doubts

At first I had my doubt that crossed with mystery
Yet I hold you dear, to listened the words you say,
You never said them clear, but you said them differently,
So when you're not there, I hear them breathe silently.

In doubt, I too fear; to repeat those words completely,
But losing fear, I may find the courage which finds you,
Abiding in knowledge unclear; in time I may define reality,
Yet still love you, and find manners have no clue.

We laughed and share memories passion and pain,
But doubt cheats on joy, and success can never rejoice,
To gain back every full moment left with that stain,
Good manners taken to make the better choice.

Having Doubts at first, I thought was hard to bear,
Until fear unclear removed the darkness into light,
And once that was done, I could walk on air,
And go where wisdom and mystery glow bright.

With no wings to fly, but if I sail towards that land,
That's when I discover doubt had no place to hide,
From courage possessing the passions that are strong,
And seem content where love defines to stay inside.

# **Earth in Upheaval**

Spiritual challenge to empower hate,
Condition of earth in upheaval,
The pendulum of torment await,
A planet disappears burning in travail.

Believers fighting without might,
They turn the right gospel page,
Into righteous path for inseparable light,
And journey to where time has no age.

The reapers came from around the bend
Cold and feverish spirit on conquest,
Eyes are distracted in the familiar wind
Persuade souls to see the pilgrim's quest.

Earth striving through the darkness,
The duller pain embraces humanity,
Forgotten in shade with tragic glances
Hope mends the bridges we form in society.

On the icy clouds where the angels went,
To moisten earth caught the air in heaven,
Peering through where sinners went,
Souls remained in a state of unforgiving

The wrath of God sends earth in upheaval
Scouring people and cities lightly departing,
With myth and prophecy binding evil,
The world loitering where a new mystery begin.

Many wait with flawed humanity,
The wrong and the right perpetuate,
Dual existence awakens the mystery,
Earth existence continues to create.

The unending perception grows,
Bringing more evil instead of goodness,
And only time and mercy knows,
How far we have gone in darkness.

Disciples of deeper realms above,
Search for gods but only one is known,
In the greater outpouring of love,
Difficult snare of finding freedom.

# Empty Promises

The smile you wore made me glad,
And promise half the world under oath,
You would give to me if riches you had,
What we could own in life or death.

Dreams climb without a pause in space,
To quicken mind and longing breathe,
Entwined around the nectar of taste,
Over soul comes power of life and death.

Those lineaments of blissful sounds,
Hidden in the whole realm of mystery,
Are they devices robed in trailing crowns?
The secrets of mind are your own fantasy.

Laden upon brave lips without fear,
From higher sphere the words are bless,
I hope to see some dreams floating in the air,
But the contents are empty promises.

You tell me the things I want to hear,
But most of them belong to eternity,
You go and come in flight and feather,
But clouds remain dark as yesterday.

# England

We are a family in England cherish land,
When I look out upon the grim houses
A sense of fear entraps the confine soul
And duty force my will to pray more earnestly,
For providence we joined the search for freedom,
Together we all have some mournful tones,
Of cage birds public concern on toiling pinion,
England pride itself with its coats of arms,
Bearing the insignia of crest and fames,
See the banner flames waving in the skies.
Although heroes may fall, they are not forgotten,
In folklore deeds written their names shall rise,
And all who dare to be brave, a crown is theirs,
Over each town their golden names will wave.
All the games of men and women our history claim
Evoke the meaning pass from parents to children,
England branches go far and reach other lands.
Our ancestry surname the winners in heraldry gain,
Their heritage lies within the walls of England.
Seeking a warmer clime upon the narrows roads,
I see the line grass of stately garden trees.
That runs through the highway of the town,
Darker stones stood out from a shadowy past
History that forms the memory that once had been,
The past unite with the present and the future.
Like footsteps hidden in the sands of time.
That is seen on either side of the dispenser,
Through which they descend to search the archives.
Beneath English lands and the trampled ground,
Nothing is lost and much more about history to gain
In the place where we lay our names can be found.

# Experience of a Lifetime

A day of fire came from the sun,
With the realm of naked flame,
Hung between the sea and the moon,
There the stars spoke my name.
And again; I find time returning,
Stood stained where the sky reign,
Experience of a lifetime burning,
Gain the path we tried to frame.
I could have run into young heaven,
With paradise wings of pure angels,
From the joy my heart was given,
Those engulf hope which love teaches.
A chance to hear mixed laughter,
And freedom chimes of celestial bells,
Link sorrow more subtle together,
Amidst trials when best efforts fails.
We climb daily higher into the sky,
That spirit Leave the past behind,
Memory of time parting the sea,
On a road set for eternity to find.
Where heaven lies earth defines,
The universities we go to search,
A lifetime we spent in demises,
Be converted into dreams reach.
The day my sins were forgiven,
A prayer from within lifted high,
The Rags and riches I had worn,
Lifetime depart deep into the sky.
Dividing darkness from my heart,
The moment a distinct world create,

The crystal glow of heavens light,
Brightens the earth where we wait.

# Fading Away

We are working for a crown,
If we fight in the battle we will win,
But we cannot just sit around,
In a cage doing nothing,
Floating down the stream of time,
Making faces like a clown.
We have not long to stay here,
And wait for all our dreams to end.
We are going down the stream,
Slowly fading away from view
Soon to breathe the last breath,
And pray that we can stay true.

# **Fading Spectator**

The loss of memory is forgotten in the wind
The moment we die before our breathe falter,
We are a fading spectator struggling to the end
And life flushes out the things we cannot alter.

Stand to surrender and wave the battered flag
On chosen fields of love and career misery
Some battles we win, but in others we drag
Our soul from the ground to unlikely victory

Taste the peace in whose arms we are thrown
In lifeline we find a rope to love and climb
Happier days of virtue spent loitering at home
Leave the cares and thoughts for others to find

We resign from the world of gaining riches
Find deeper sense of peace and happiness.

# Family memories

Memories are with me night and day,
But the ones that means the most to me,
Wherever I go, are those of my family?
And always known must leave for others to see.

I count the months and they turned into days,
I count the days and they turned into weeks,
I count the weeks and they turned into minutes,
Each time I count the memories; there are more intrigues.

From the colour of clothes adorn and meekly worn,
To hay high grass frolicking in the garden,
We hide in postural shade from the burning sun,
And roll and play beneath the rustling green.

Looking up into the sky at lights deeper than dept,
And wishing upon a star for a new fond dream,
To come true with virtue clean enough to sweep,
Our hopes so high, we could look down from heaven.

Through the worlds we gaze hoping to find,
Love in summer, and pleasure wrap up warm in winter,
Within the memories which pierce our mind,
Are those we love more than what we remember.

# <u>Farewell</u>

I was not there in time to say farewell,
Or hold you so close to love, till my heart tires,
I was too late when I came, anguish had already fell,
And hoist the pain to smear the sum of fears.

Farewell is a lonely word clandestine in the wind,
Begin a journey and end a phenomenon being,
Where the thoughts stay long enough to be kind,
And images and shadows continue loitering.

On the precipice of time where we once roam,
In bliss and solitude, till darkness covers the road,
Farewell my lovely, our parting is from this home,
But you have begun a crusade on the highest road.

# Final day of years

Pain came in the place where years had stood
Unaffected by new hazards and old traumas,
Engulfing dreams we had when times were good,
Counting the cost and the sum total life gross.

Old and cold hands hold the trembling crown,
We finally fold them in peace at recluse ease
From preying eyes no longer society's burden
We find our niche kneel deep where God see.

Time outlived the careers that was chosen
Woven in sombre moods the paths we cross,
Doubt cast dark clouds over the chilly terrain
Soak damp plains to make them slippery places.

My final days of years came along in rapid flight,
Moving passion and desire away into fatigue realm,
From lust to dust no eyes to see the fading light,
Darkness steals the pleasure in sight of my dream.

Leave burned out flames in cooler flashes
Dashing complain of ailing aches and pains,
Not the fantasy of adventures lifetime carries
Worn torch illuminate the souls awing reins.

We'll shine again while pass from earth atmosphere
Deeds acclaimed to be heavens celestial calling,
Guide ancient path we have forth and sought over
Till in final years there will be no more travelling.

# Flowers

Flowers express our internal feelings,
Priceless gift given to someone special
Wrapped in new colours when love begins,
On such occasions sends a message of good will.

Country style flowers may take time to handpick,
Emotions in personal thoughts allow you the choice,
To reach love ones with the right bouquet,
Flowers can do wonders to help surprised voice.

When you attempt the task and think you're too late
Take a moment and order the flowers,
Sitting at home or on the phone they will compensate
Services rendered with gratitude and memories.

Reach in time the requiem for a final journey,
Aspects of our minds stay within living confines
Flowers create inspiration of our personality,
On mother's day the blossoms finds modern verities.

Because it can show your love on different occasions,
Valentines symbolism of weddings and elegance
Flowers stand out from the crowd for graduations,
Take flowers if you want celebrate birthday and romance.

# <u>Fragrant Of My Heart</u>

Scooping up the dyed pieces dried stiff,
From the burning sun that is yet young,
Swift time command that nothing be lost,
And took faith to where the wind has blown.

Our dreams and hopes away from the course,
To collect all the fragments our thoughts own,
In burning pain, when residue silence eclipse,
The forlorn path our marred visage has worn.

We look at defeat with pools of citadel eyes,
Arch back determine to complete the sentence,
And remember how love was like a daunting quiz,
Where youthful time and words made no sense.

And having found too, my heart was broken,
Just as those brunt pieces became blunt,
I stoop to mend, in borrowed feelings began,
Slowly to collect the fragments of my heart.

And close emotions where other doors open,
For a new entrance into my shrouded soul,
Betrayal bruises the air with every breath taken,
Fragments of our lives throughout the world.

Trail with participle phrase and Reciprocate,
Against the wretched barriers and angry fire,
In lonely afterthought pain fixes the subordinate,
Until winding time became the only obvious healer.

# **<u>Freedom Comes</u>**

Greed has torn off society sparkling wings,
Fleeing the ugliness that resides within,
Society sees the desperate conditions?
That humanity is muddled up in.

What is so sweet that life is all about sin?
Without faith freedom is incomplete,
Right from wrong we even can't explain,
We miss much and cry too late.

With conscience out of life we can tell,
Another person anything that's on our mind,
And know that all nationalities has free will,
Till their inept culture is refine.

From sore throat right down into the soul,
New age wants to free man from his pain,
But I see stain windows continue to control,
Redemption on man the things of sin.

That reverberates and goes deep within,
Many have not changed their heart,
Only changed membership to begin,
Where association left blank space to start.

Freedom waits at every mans gate,
Hopes get closer when a path is bending,
We are possess by the things we hate,
But leave only thoughtful prints in the wind.

# **Gathering Dust**

They sink into the ground with silence,
Voices we'll never hear making a sound,
Only wishful smiles appear in a trance,
Gathering dust where the names are found.

They cannot rise from the deep isles,
To raise a smile even to murmur a sigh,
More darkness pours into the abyss,
Sunlight has closed time against the sky.

Idle flowers bowed in quiet solitude,
Left to revive by the morning early dew,
Flatten with footprints walked in tribute,
Push the hollow ground from distant view.

There they lay on bed of silent dismay,
Awaiting eternity, bodies gathering dust,
Old moss and rocks cover the mystery,
The verdant grass becomes a blanket of rust.

In disguise spirit rise to fly like an arrow,
Leaving the resting place to gather dust,
They may return as forces in a shadow,
And walk over grass where they lay the host.

# **Glimpse of Heaven**

Love can be glimpse of heaven,
With no sand castles or moon dunes,
Floating beneath the brooding sun,
No politicians or shopping trolleys.
I want to see who made the moon,
Hung the stars on a curtain of dreams,
Left behind the crucifix coins we wear.
Even the cripple have a triple crown
The lame leap with dances in a song,
Going to see a king on wings of prayer,
Indulgencies of the weak can be strong,
Bind the death howls and smearing fire.
Exchange miracles borne amongst angels,
Moon beams spread the tapestry of heaven.
The kingdom come over every tropical isle,
Praises flung with jewel beads in the air,
And live on whatever Gods grace brings.
Bare the nature and the invisible power,
Life will be peaceful; we can play and sing,
Heavens jubilee innumerable company,
With stars to guide the beauty of the night,
They paint the sky in a transparent ring.
Speeding arrows engulf with showers,
Holy Grail shine in the sky stained light,
A halo makes a road on the celestial trail.
The rising sun sees another day unveil,
No night of sorrow to drape with fears,
The curse of sin gone with unfriendly realm.
In early dew strung the ephemeral intent,
Dotted in houses where there was no room,

Robe with immortality to split the firmament.
Rising humans leave the empty tomb,
Forgiven words left with fleeting kisses,
Rapture saints the immortal tapestry given.
Tribulation disguise drop a star in the abyss,
Splattered garland around the throne,
And we see only faint glimpse of heaven.

# God's Assurance

After spending so many years in the wilderness
God's assurance is that He will be with us,
Many of us also look at our own inadequacy,
And live every day in despondency.
Sometimes broken and humbled,
What's the only thing we really need?
It is God's assurance that he will be with us
Never forsake or leave us in a mess.
Many of us also look at our own failures
And doubt that God could possibly cares
God can see us through the rubble,
But we hide ourselves in times of trouble.
He wants us victorious over every hurdle,
Climb the highest mountain and walk in the valley,
He desires to deliver us so that we may live free,
Free of sin, free of guilt, free to choose our destiny.

# Going where dreams go

But I am going where dreams go
With old acquaintance converge
To leave a vestige of thought aglow
As you too shall adore, more, and more
Pictures, places and lives will emerge.
For if this year should quickly leave,
Some will sigh while others may grieve.
But if we forget and, and afterwards remember
The things that made us laugh and dance,
In time, the memories will rearrange
Shadows rising from the ashes, in realm of peace.
The future will not look bleak and appear strange
In just another breath we'll be gone
And the worlds will be caught in a trance,
Joy in our eyes will appear to advance.
When a new road is paved
Not with gold, or merchandise we can hold,
But to share the privilege of grace
And all the things we desire to know,
Are found inside the place where dreams go.

# Gold within the soul

I have received your loved, and feel secure,
A paradox opposite the world made of pure gold.
Your passion that I feel peaceful and demure
Be a part of you tonight to have and to hold.

Finding greater riches then that of diamonds,
There is gold within the soul
And greater ore feelings demands
Make our destiny to take control.

The boundaries are pushed aside,
New territories unfold the exploration
Deploy where there is no place to hide
The creative realm acquired mission.

# Great is The Son

Great is the Son when his work is done
Heavens portals are lifted up
They will be done on earth as in heaven
He goes wide through the celestial gates
Be ye lifted up you everlasting doors
And let the king of glory come in
Jesus meets the angels who are with him
We behold the ancient days.

The firmament paint repose
Every flower and trees in the garden,
Glitter and shine like a terrestrial rose.
All the gold we find in the ground,
They were made by the great Son,
Fashion among human took our sin
And in him we have found God.

Great is the son who binds the cool shade
In the night slips the light around the world,
He makes us not afraid,
To walk in a world of darkness,
Because he is the everlasting light
Shining through the key hole of our heart.

# Good Grief

When friends have gone, memories shall not,
Be unkind as the fragrant flowers that fade,
With vast images moving hands and foot,
And sinking through into where grief reside.

Within the mind, emotions overwhelm and define,
Streams moving slowly in pitiless winding flow,
And take each drop of darkness beyond time,
To heal under rainy clouds made of sorrow.

Passing the source illusion of heart has taken,
The loved given to all; and love left alone,
In clouds that took sorrow could not be awaken,
To signs of grieving until grieving is done.

Then feelings awake to cope with the pain,
Having patiently waited for the release day,
When joy resonate will come resolute again,
And grief floats in the clouds away.

If there be swords that tears the heart open,
And leave bitter scares of inescapable reality,
To numb the existence of human being,
It is the vulnerability of grief in our society.

# Grow Me Up With Love

Grow me up with verses of love,
And endless strength emerges,
You have made life possible to move,
My heart into where the road converges.

Grow me up in the language of love,
And be an emblem of forgiveness,
Give value from kingdoms above,
Prayer that makes life becomes bliss.

These are thoughts on a worn path,
I love the beautiful soul within,
None can kill the fire in my heart,
Reside in the gloom and in the dim.

We're on our way to that heaven,
We're going to meet guardian angels,
We can hear heavenly bells ringing,
We're not far from our loved ones.

# Heaven

In comfort, heaven is still the best
Place to go after we come to the end,
You and I will go home to rest,
And pass the test that God has sent.

We'll be missing for little awhile
But leave a fragrant taste in friends mind,
By the disappearing lingering smile,
The name absorbs the memory for a time.

In pictures we see a shadow in the well
Of the person that could have given
A greater contribution for others to tell
Mankind about their dream of heaven.

When earth cease to intrigue the spirit
We will join millions of enlightened stars
Pass through the sun without the heat
Wave at the moon and walk upon mars.

See another world filled with surprise
Old and young share the same terrain,
We commune on the other side of paradise
The destiny that makes us young again.

# <u>Heaven and Earth</u>

God created heaven and earth
We were the fashion renew,
God was the creator from birth,
And the sky was also new.

We only knew heaven was higher
Stretched far into unending distance,
Beginning our life and character,
The discovery brought new science.

Created in the celestial realm,
The strong and the weak with strength,
The embryo of transplant intent began,
To oblige the soul in unknown might.

Beautiful colours in nature entrenched,
Hopes springs Gods eternal grace,
Begin the mortal race on a bizarre road,
With new creation of continuous race.

Cold calculated chaos began misgiving,
In the beginning opulence was lost,
Temptation found refuge sauntering,
To the existence of penitent cost.

Mankind suffer rejection and abuse,
Pride took a ride in ungainly pursuit,
To reconstruct the skills we once refuse,
But could not make earth a safer retreat.

# Heavenly Father

My father is in heaven just waiting for me,
Preparing a unique place of rest for tomorrow,
And when I get there how happy I will be,
In my flight of joy there will be no more sorrow.

When I take a heavenly star to go through the air,
In paradise on streets of gold other people will walk,
And I will know the change in the atmosphere,
Just been there without street lamps for it is not dark.

Pull up in my dream the sheets of celestial lights,
Eternity riding high on the firmament of stain glass,
New life erase the guilt that own the quibbling past,
No moon ice or winter spring hanging over the cities.

My father is in heaven away from this besotted time,
His anxious blood runs deep through my veins,
I can feel him in my body; see him in my mind,
Gauge the cosmic realm to define the species.

In time, in memory, we return to the cradle of love,
The father we worship, the king we strongly adore,
Alpha and Omega, the exceptional being from above,
A father's love is the key that opens every door.

Mine inescapable failure made into a testimony,
Onwards and upwards made a way to meet his wave,
I am almost going home soon no reason to worry,
Outliving the impact the one for my life he gave.

# **Heavenly sunset**

Summer sunset
Drying the wet dew
From between the shivering grass
A blade of earth reopened
Morning shadows renewed
The hush of the sauntering wind
Clench consummate air in our hand
Movements of trees singing
With Restless whispering
They know secrets that are hidden
Something echoed in the wind
A force came from above the placid sky
Unrecognized message our eyes deny
The sudden shock fell silent upon our lips
Like thunder touching the leaves
A frail breeze calmly disguises
Swept souls into heavenly paradise
To see angels, old friends and even Jesus
Leaving laughter to find another sunset
Heavenly sunset sometimes your eyes are wet
With the tears of our best friends
Look through the long treasured years
Remind yourself that pain was only a light fear
And see the happiness you gave
You were the one we love
In songs and testimonies share
Your memories made us all happier
Uniting distant broken spirit
Sharing hopes and regret
The past comforting the present
Our dreams put reality back together

We embrace our lost with each other
Forgiveness taught us all a lesson

Now you are gone
A new day ushered in another song
Into the heavenly sunset
To meet redemption's best
Take your wings and fly to the top
Of heavens highest mountain and look down
You will see us making plans
We will mark the last rites you took
Scattering ashes beyond the grass bank
Only a fragrance beneath the rich earth
Back to the place of your birth
But memories will live out the season
Cheered on by your angelic presence
We hold the hand of the celestial choice
Fate had made for us with forlorn tears
Finally facing up to the sum of fears
The moment we all had dreaded
When for the last time we would meet
Trying to hold back every second into minute
Cherishing your memory along the way
Remembering the events of each day
Wishing family in your unrepentant prayer
The sudden departure drew us all closer
To preserve love in peaceful beauty
With sunset sharing your shadow
Your soul walks over the morning dew
From where you came at birth
And found the spirit to take you gloriously
Into heavenly eternity

# <u>Hope</u>

Hope is the fondest word I know,
Which starts opening new windows?
The mind echoes with its peculiar glow
Another breeze removes doubtful shadows.

Hope can always travel into the distance
Refuse to let go of desire and intrigue,
Takes chances with the wind in romance,
And make occasions becomes unique.

Rage it knows only in the quest bestow,
Endurance through softening words,
From the gentle hearts it will quietly flow,
Patient finds refuge in secret it holds.

And seldom will it let you down
For the world knows it dares not lose hope,
When our dreams are still unknown,
We hold unto the rope on every slippery slope.

Till the cause begin to flee over distant hill,
Opportunity ends and defeat as friends
The pride, the power and fearful thrill,
Of memories traded in soften winds.

# Hope Regain

Her sapphire eyes penetrated my soul,
Water of a full cup flowing from inside
Smeared her face with the bitter cold,
Streams of fresh joy could not hide.

The thing which made smiles sparkling
Began the bliss within
From excitement of being
Strangely in love again

Bittersweet tears are softly torn,
From reflection glistens off her face
Betrayed the fate she had worn,
Breathless sleep hidden by grace.

From love lost to hope regain,
The flame of Poison taste,
Disappear with the whisper of pain
And silence pierces the cruel place.

# House of Mirrors

Most ambition starts with a dream,
And never ends when the night brings,
A wicked thought in a natural stream,
Fantasy is not seen when the alarm bell rings.

The chimes of reality try to awake you,
But you are lost where pain can't be seen,
And correction is too hard for heart to renew,
Everyone you thought was so highly esteem.

Some wore terror, others brought boredom,
Come to use you for another adventure,
Duplicity is a two edge sword of persecution,
And carries a frown reflected in the mirror.

We can always find time to laugh or weep,
Bliss, marriage, occupation appear discreet,
When the pieces are broken they cut deep,
And the mourners go about the street.

A house of mirrors has broken cracks,
They widen and will not procrastinate forever,
Before shattering into small magic pieces,
And the original beauty is lost altogether.

Most fearful dreams appear in a nightmare,
The puzzling prize penetrating the mind,
But it's not the terror you and I should fear,
Rather, the Apocalypse of another kind.

# <u>Humanity</u>

Applying aspiration and disillusion,
Modernism exhibit blissful mirth,
In commerce and religious myth,
Society is drunk with the age of sexual duplicity,
Dismissive of all moral chastity,
The compelling gaze of humanity,
Driving nations further into the fog,
Preparing for Armageddon like maggots,
Eating away rotten minds from the core
Earth lay sparkling on the fire.
Tarnished with desire burning with desire,
Goodness and mercy sipping from the cup,
This forgotten age of humanity is burning up,
Pleasure fleeing faster than light,
Individuals losing the bewildered fight.
Depravity of humanism rising higher,
Global temperature getting warmer,
Bringing to roost end time explosion,
Couple with terror and derelict derision,
Sensing the past has no future obligation.
People with baggage, misplace from every nation,
Find their way to wealthier lands,
Hordes covered the clouds like sand,
The result of mixed community,
Swamp the forgotten age of beauty,
With lesser grace darkening prosperity,
Mere time looks upon humans kindly,
With the compelling gaze of mystery.

# <u>I Am Pressing On</u>

The closer I get to heaven
Pressing on the upward way,
The less of earth is seen.
Spinning into a new day,
With the cross before me,
And my soul has fully turn,
Baptized in the Holy Spirit,
Walking daily with heart burn,
I put the world behind me.
Pressing on to higher ground,
Climbing above the trees,
I am leaving this old world.
The grief and the bed of fleas,
Forfeit the game of pride,
For more time on my knees,
The mystery of joy cannot hide.
The blessings contained inside,
I count the years as months,
And the month as just a minute,
Counting down the seconds,
And it will be any moment now,
I'll touch the heavenly summit.

# I don't know why

On a day like today,
The heaven is soft with dew,
And in trees; birds have eyes crying,
But the air up in the sky was new.

With poppy clouds looking down,
From the broken road out of heaven,
Upon fine lines and pleasant farm,
A blanket of trees canvasses the ground.

There were farmers and shepherds,
Harvesting in the same field,
I don't know why the work was so hard?
Raking the soil and planting seed.

Shepherds find the grassy verge,
Where life is quiet and only soft birds sing,
In trees where they rest and observe,
The broken road to heaven.

# <u>I know who I am</u>

I know who I am
I am a child
I am a mysterious man
I am a special friend

I am sinner
I am significant,
I am redeem forever
I am a saint

I am forgiven
I am loved
I am not ashamed
I am accepted by God

I am going to another level
I am healed
I am here when you call
I am here to worship

I am bought with a price
I am given new life
I am learning to be wise
I am alive

I am the portrait who sees
I am a mysterious man
I am a personal witness
I know who I am

I am light and darkness converge

I am a citizen
I am a sojourner on earth
I am going to heaven

I am the person you will remember
I am always in your presence
I am a character
I am free to roam the universe

# <u>I Thought I Could Love You</u>

I thought I could love you,
It was inspiration I spent not knowing,
But perceive that every notion was true,
Meander through the existence of time.

There was a moment of loving you more,
When you and each image brought a sigh,
I had inspiration which made illusion appear,
So near yet indefinite reality could not apply.

The feeling of so much love driven to control,
A jewel stole to build a palace of bliss,
Eternity could not be long enough to hold,
The wonderful thought appears so precious.

Words of truth I know, because it meant much,
Simply wonderful for such thought to exist,
The tears of utter joy I could almost touch,
Among the fairground treat the soul entreat.

I thought I could love you in that perfect dream,
Others found a way the yearning to forget,
As I fail, whole life shame goes into the stream,
Moved on and build up greater walls to protect.

# I Will Live

I will not live on public feelings,
Or on consensus of large masses,
But I will live with strong feelings,
Been here among the godless classes.
With life itself to be held accountable,
I shall neither die; nor heaven be denied.
But I shall live amides the trouble,
And if I should decide to get even.
It will be with believers of another realm,
And not join hands with the deplorable;
Although some friends will complain,
In the faith that once was adorable.
And while pleasure from earth is extracted,
Where the sting of that maliciousness is gathering,
The ethnicity of mankind's interest is contracted,
In the value of pride for their nation.
From memories the echoes keep sounding
Having live in the past, I will abide in the future,
By the laws of grace abounding,
I will live where danger enrages the howling fire
And human passion keeps on burning,
With the torrid flames spreading higher,
As hostilities on earth keeps on churning,
The race to leave keeps nation warring.

# Ice Cream

In the hive of events and concessions,
Ice cream combines with our daily indulgence,
At fetes and fairs and lardy wedding exhibitions,
Churned rich cream is mixed with the service.

Rum and raisins even fruit and nutty pistachio,
Folding finish soft texture ingredients ends dizzily,
Your experience can find young generations aglow
Consuming lashes of breathtaking quality.

Luxury pieces and crunchier toffee chunks melting,
In the parlour, desires tore through our passion,
And we like nothing better than the great enriching
We get when it comes from eating ice cream.

The perfect taste softens the temperature
Fondant cream and sugar spectrum infuse the flavour.

# I've got you

I've got you right here
Running through my mind,
Towards the finish line yet unclear,
Advancing with the threads of time.

Shadows of your love coming nearer,
To the labyrinth where hopes unwind,
I've got you serenading into my ear,
Piercing tune with stitches that bind.

My soul to yours sweetly entwined,
Upon a road paved with bliss to burst,
In splendour we'll embrace a life sublime,
And love each other into fading dust.

When day has worn away towards sunset,
I've got you when the nights turn cold,
Having formed by minds our liquid asset,
You are greater value than paved gold.

I've got you sharing every moment's success,
When pain has turn and triumph over failure;
I've got you with all those endearing riches,
But can this wealth be such a crime to fear?

# I'll miss you

I'll miss you, when you have gone missing
From my heart, and I hear only the hissing sigh,
Leaping gently out of the air with mourning,
And lament from the void inside of me.

I'll let memories assail and climb,
Taking promises drawn on the trail of love,
In time, winding further down into my mind,
All the dreams cost sorrows to grieve.

And when you're gone let time play for us,
In shinning sleep the songs we love to sing,
In our golden days, we embrace the trail with bliss,
And every tender kiss was as green.

As the grass upon which we turn and lay,
And hay became a blanket upon the ground,
I'll miss you every night, and every daunting day,
Even in dreams which make no sound.

Going high around the sun and under the stars,
I see the birth of a shinning new place,
Where we will be inseparable from our dreams,
And tears following you out will no longer be trace.

# **I'm here**

I'm here; I thought you were my best friend,
But I found out too late,
You only pretend,
So I am left here with pains and ache.

I'm here left on the empty shelf,
With no reply and too many questions,
Trying hard to come to myself,
Staring at the wall and finding reasons.

It seems like nothing I did was good,
My esteem slips below self worth,
For me, love was blind,
So I'm just here all by myself.

Getting lonelier and passing time,
Hoping for a thought to guide me,
To a place I've never been,
And plunge me through the veil of victory.

Or Must I just stay here and quietly give up?
If better luck comes from outside,
I'm here with an optimism look,
Ready to make the sacrifice,

And give human kind another chance,
For love to come and fill my desire,
And even take the place,
That is low and lonelier

# I'm in Heaven with You

I'm in heaven with you,
Spirited away on a burning sphere,
Inside of me are the new
Imprints of this adventure.


You came like a dream from above,
Then the world change suddenly,
And the things you love,
I will take with me into eternity.

Love joy and peace,
Each emotion with its own truth,
Holding you in close embrace,
Feels like the new birth.

You are here the breath,
And consciousness of my being,
Transported on a paradise wreath,
Into divinity of angelic realm.

I'm in heaven where my soul is alive,
This earthly feeling never existed before,
In God I do believe,
We were meant to be with each other.

# Immaculate Women

The choices make a vast difference,
If they live for others or for themselves,
Driven by character or the opulence of chance,
Immaculate women grant only glimpses.

We only see but the faint shadows of her beauty,
And her inner qualities are only guessed at,
To conformed the soul has denied certain reality,
A place in society is the stepping stone to react.

To make the right choice, choosing not to lose,
Begin a journey and end a phenomenon being,
Live as close to love to smear the sum of fears,
Give hope for comfort and help to cope with pain.

Her heart wish to tell a tale and tear you away,
From the pain all the things that make you ache,
And seldom will her love forsake or go astray,
While nothing you do can equal hate.

Love blooms where great passion fills the heart,
And her beauty overwhelms the world in fantasy,
As sunshine emanates amides the tearful spirit,
Fear fades and softens the path to eternity.

And lay agony across the mortal reins,
A kiss of death wrap around the inner being,
Like dreams that soak the sheets in tearful rains,
Immaculate women sweet and highly esteem.

Where bliss and solitude richer treasures found,
The synergy of smile is existence with reason,

For emotions to be clandestine in the wind,
Of all God's creation, out of many such inspiration.

# <u>Immortality</u>

Heaven is above the light of the lording sky,
Among stars, I see a different place stands adrift,
Where my weary shadow will find immortality,
Silently in solemn praise awaits the night,

And gusty voices sang where the soul cry high,
May call a man out of a small mouse hole,
To lay his soul naked beneath the cold moist sky,
In silent murmur sleep the calm the weary soul.

With Gods peace inspiring each tentative step,
The birth of new horizon contrast the present,
The wisdom of god is our greatest help,
He will never ask you to do anything indecent.

Behind closed doors the immorality starts,
Sleeping with the code that let them live together,
Strangers become friends but are still far apart,
Can easily become friends but finds it hard to be lover.

# In Our Lives

In our lives, past and present,
We had ignorance untold,
And the virus was unpleasant,
It releases dangers we could not hold.
On the path of injustice and inequality,
And revelation that had to show,
Enlightenment before reaching our destiny,
On that widening road of tomorrow.

But however dark the night may be,
The darkness leaves more mystery,
Surrounding the centuries that smudges history.
And the curses do not seem to fade away,
As fast as blessings come infrequently.

The torment keeps on clinging,
With such ominous numbing fear,
Of dangers that the future may be bring,
We see through a glass darkly obstacles unclear.
Unstable people waver when facing the truth,
But only one Christ can be our savoir,
We were already doom from birth,
Cast in with the lords despise few to be delivering.

Out of the realm of sad destitute,
Into the splendour of a marvellous light,
That every human possess flesh and spirit,
Our lives are a beacon in the night.
Responsibility falls on every individual,
Perhaps heaven will not be denied.
When choosing what will be held accountable,

In our lives we get the chance to decide,
Nothing is impossible or insurmountable.

## **<u>In passing</u>**

I pass by your house today,
And in passing I saw your shadow appear,
Then turn as if to stay, and half disappear,
Retreat slowly away.

As if in haste you had to go,
And may seek to find another illusive time,
Opportunity to come again into my mind,
If passing the same way tomorrow.

You leave the vestment of your shadow,
To perfumed the air,
And if the thoughts I have of you should go,
And wearily disappear.

I will remember when I grieve,
That you were distinctly here,
Passing amidst the realm I leave,
To turn in silence and upon your beauty stare.

To think about the shadow I have seen,
And all the sleepless hours through the night,
Your shadow reflect the moonlight,
Of the vision that should have been in my dream.

I will arise and come to you softly again,
Passing by your house in the patient breeze,
And in darkness, I shall have some peace,
When I see you as you were in my dream.

# <u>In the beginning</u>

In the beginning we never knew teardrops,
We were the fashion becoming new,
God's creation brought the raindrops,
And the sky in heaven turned blue.

We only knew the innocence of gender,
Stretched far back into unbending distance,
Beginning our characteristics and behaviour,
The experiment brought new science.

Paused in the realm; waiting for life to begin,
Something's in weakness can be strength,
The embryo of transplant intent stood waiting,
To oblige in the steps of unknown spirit.

Jagged thoughts in age more entrenched,
But hopes springs the proposing grace,
Begin the twist of nature on a bizarre road,
With new creation of continuous race.

Cold calculated chaos began misgiving,
In the beginning opulence was lost,
Temptation found refuge surrendering,
To the existence of a pertinent cost.

Creation suffer rejection and abuse,
And took a ride in ungainly pursuit,
To reconstruct the skills once refuse,
But could not make earth a safer retrea

# In the dark

I am on the darkest street,
Left alone to find my way out,
All steps are trodden in black,
Taking the thoughts into visible light.

I will take the narrow road,
Leading to where I want to go,
If the road I take is too dark and old,
Then I will take the new and walk slow.

If I can hardly see where to walk,
And go where the winding streets go,
I will watch for the white chalk,
Piercing the dark like an arrow.

Although the sun is bright,
In the dark abyss secret motive lies,
Hidden causes not found out,
Remained as unsolved mysteries.

If the road we are on is the darkest way,
Better tread softly until you can wait,
Until when the darkness goes away,
Taken from all the troubles we make.

# <u>Inside Paradise</u>

Inside our soul among the glittering choice,
Lives unconquered morality in versatile mind,
We can all find our voice to tell others about paradise,
With inspiration and reasons we don't understand.

Sow experience in the names we give to our mistakes,
Intrinsic pictures beautiful and delicate remained exquisite,
Dreams known by shapes in shadows of poignant images,
It feels like paradise in side where the taste is private.

Cordial pilgrimages were invariably in a state of two minds
Sophistication of time where opportunity is left to design,
A more enviable world magnificent by mortal standards,
Those better pursuits of mind taking up the confine.

We struggle to conceal the valiant buildings inside
Excel in every intense wind the atmosphere can supply,
Our venture for charm and enchantment to step outside,
Unaware of indefinite failure waiting to grinned horribly.

We are pleasant inside when we get over difficulties,
Open wide the state of vitality in appearance of paradise,
Shredded in base seclusion we conceive secret dignities,
Bruised like flowers in the wind without expressive voices.

Fallen in places the consciousness of dark creases,
The sense that we are not alone in the cradle of emotion,
We are deeper in love with the imagination of promises,
And we hide the reliable facts with jealous suspicion.

# January

Start wooing with all the clocks chiming,
Slip the slippery seconds around earth,
And dance with the skies in celebration,
All from pulse to breathe, and to new birth.

January, the first light of another year,
And the glory of that maiden orbit,
Wake silently from golden dust to appear,
A long time coming; we had known it.

After taking down the decorations,
Give chances for the changing course,
To breathe New Year's resolutions,
And as it grows, given hope a chance.

A brimful of dreams watches all doors opens,
Letting hope in and visions lets out more,
But so long as January defines what begins,
 It has the key to mingle with pleasure.

 January stands steep in splendour passing by,
Spectra of the seasons towering head,
And hung the gem of lights to guide the sky,
With stars bright and glittering away they fled.

And float midway in opportunity abound,
To such deep measure on thrushes of rapture,
Upon fair winds January is known in all the land,
 From drifts to snowy clefts and sunny sphere.

The wakening realm will come back again,
And life begins new through cold and death,
January is the beginning of the end,
Round the islands it goes in triumphant rebirth.

# Last rites

An hour after been at the church,
With others standing who was sad,
I did not know they cared so much,
As others saw; the blessings I had.

But into my world they could not look,
For my sorrow could not be awaken,
By the last rites from a common book,
And bring myself to stop crying.

My soul sought the loss to be forgiven,
All that I loved; had suddenly gone,
While my heart was still breaking,
Life moved on leaving me forsaken.

In my thoughts, darker clouds surround,
When the final rites was solemnly given,
Ashes go from view down into the ground,
With dept of good will waiting the rest of heaven.

Time may rolled a torrent of memories within,
To draw a glint of sun from this stormy life,
And the fear in death shall lose its sting,
And we prepare better to meet our fate.

# **<u>Lasting Hopes</u>**

May the summer love and joy,
Warm your heart and home,
Bring the humour you have deploy,
Following where your spirit roam.

With lasting hopes that will endure,
Through all the passing seasons,
And virtue bring out the best in you,
The qualities share with friends.

There is much more love reside in you,
Lasting hopes can make the difference,
When celebrating something incredibly new,
There is joy and laughter in your presence.

With the earthly eyes you have seen,
A greater new world transformed,
With the twinkling of an eye opening,
These earthen treasures are renewed.

No longer confine nor to a sickness resign,
There is plenty to bless you in this world,
With time enough to leave this realm,
And send the spirit back to God.

# Lean On God

Praise God in the good times
Praise God in the bad times
Praise God when the sun shines
Praise God at all times

In pain when we have sorrow
There is hope for tomorrow
In time, faith will grow
Our testimony others will know

God's love is hope for the world
The everlasting destiny for our soul
When there is no one to hold
We can lean on God for he is in control

# Life overcomes death

Life overcomes death,
When Lent of days began
To proclaim better health
From the power we had gain.

Over in pharaohs land,
Where dreams began,
Mercy stood inspired upon the sand
Shout the acclamation.

Life had where death once roam
Stole time and strength
Agony in the hearts of every man
Beat with every hopeful breath.

In pain and bitter grief,
Tired feet free from the cage
Praise time that had them relief
Life brings freedom to the age.

Many were smitten
By a force they could not see
Refugees fleeing from the awful condition,
Death passes over the sea.

By angelic hand moving along
The strong man screaming children and women
Fearful thrill voices command
Choice of life is given to everyone.

# Little Troubles

We disagree and everything goes black,
When I am down and cannot get back,
It feels like I have lost virtue deep inside,
Which may go wandering beyond the outside?
When my pride is hurt it beats in my heart,
The attack of rejection trying to pull us apart,
With some dejected feelings of emotion,
We are both worse off than when we began.
We have entered the realm of another reality,
Little troubles look big but they are really silly.
No matter how hard we may fall down the hill,
We can climb back on our feet and do well.
And if it makes us feel better about ourselves,
Then we can defeat all these little troubles.
And don't take the cares of this life as a curse;
Try to make the most when things seem worse.
It takes time and courage to be strong,
To go along we earn the prize to get along.
Our heart may be breaking with sorrow inside
But there is a smile of joy we cannot hide.

The reality of it goes silent back in with a grin
Although secretly our hearts are breaking.
We can keep warm by love and desire.
Some laughs we have are taking us higher.

# Losing Society

Unrestricted but refined and free,
There was a crashing sound at the gate,
We are all look round for a place to flee
But our reaction has too late.

The biggest fault we find in losing society
Is getting to the bottom of self centeredness,
Sin is the problem nations are facing today,
Elements reinforce by, drugs, rapes and robberies.

The whole world is driven to despair,
Cultural differences provides the epidemic,
Promote separatism and treat others so unfair,
We respond to issues and start to panic.

Losing faith in our ability to influence relationship,
And make society a better offer of partnership.

# Love and darkness

I am facing love and darkness in sin
My heart rages loudly for atonement,
But the aching agony goes long and deep within,
They fly swift to wounded region.

I am walking blind in a tunnel of dark,
What will ignite new hope in dreams where it began?
My awaken soul tries to leap into mythical spark,
Burning desire with every passion imagine.

Fear let go in marvelled wander and I travel far
Staying near the walk of faith, but doing what I hate,
The burning love of anger grows even stronger,
This flame in the dark is burning the brightest.

Electric fire, passion desire glowing in the night,
Burning flame human pain reveals another dark realm
Light consumes darkness and makes the day look bright
There is a love binding me to earth and it shines in heaven.

As angelic lamplights Passover on the vacant street,
Jostling the flames of freedom forcing our conscience,
To explore time and consume the darkness we meet,
This love for earth is a reality to illuminate doubtful science.
Love and darkness, dwells within our heart
In shady light, seasons embrace both phenomenons
That exists within the crater of twilight mist,
And can disappear just as quickly as they came.

# Love Builds the Bridge

The years went by and I went along
I tried to run but now I can hardly stand
We watched as children were born
Love builds the bridge
And I felt the change
Between your heart and mine

When joy came
We sometimes acted like clowns
Ending up smiling and loosing the frown
Disappointment brought us to the ground

Romance was a chance
Dreams disappear into the distance
Cruel emotions twisting my soul into a trance

God stood by like an angel in disguise
Turning our little home into happier times
Life is full of love again
Praise God for the miracle amidst the pain

# **Love Delay**

O love delay, wherever you are?
I was searching for you in vain
You are the only thing I am waiting for
To take away this aching pain.

I should have pluck up courage long ago
But now I will grow old in hope of finding,
Images peering through the window,
Transition hides me away from everything.

Where is the balm for my healing?
Like something missing out of my dream,
That wakes up very late in the morning,
I stayed where I was waiting for the alarm.

Love delayed answers to mixed request,
In order to mould and shape our desires,
Confidence grows as we learn to invest,
And strengthen our faith in prayers.

Time did not mare our beautiful character,
Nor was hope lost in love's seeming delay,
Patient was counted for greater honour,
Not our selfish wants to be on display.

# Love is

Perfect love cast out fear,
Love is in the eyes of a dear friend,
Love is found transformed in the air,
True love has no boundaries to end.

Love is in every moment we pause,
Love leaves an imprint in our heart,
Love covers distance and show the cause,
Love is a world full of charming delight.

This is love in tears and blazing laughter,
Love shines radiantly on our faces,
Love struggles and overcomes despair,
Love is the sweetest emotions our lips can taste.

Love is icy winter and lazy summer days,
Love is celebrated in great victory parade,
Love is in photographs with a million memories,
Love is nations treasures hid in peaceful shade.

Love is forgiving your enemies instead of hate,
Love is the first appearance of a new born child,
Love is precious, and far too costly to waste,
Let us share this unique gift we all have inside.

# Love Is the Heart Beat of the Soul

She whispers a melody to me softly,
Her words clutch my heart with passion,
Heartbeat of conscience finding the mystery,
Of body and soul entwined with the emotion.

The inky stars glow bright over the waters,
And we are transforming into a life of bliss,
To make our reflections like heavenly figures,
Covering eyes and lips with pearly riches.

My inner thoughts sparkled while listening,
To the spirit lifted with every heartbeat,
Comfort in the fondest path and decisions taken,
Love is the key that makes our life complete.

We who were nothing have become something,
More important than mere existence,
We feel the heartbeat of each other's suffering,
To share the things upon our conscience.

Every heartbeat is a splendid life line,
Where Love is keeps the soul breathing,
Every beat sends a message to define,
The reasons we keep on believing.

# **Man and Woman**

In time, God created man and woman
We were the earthly fashion renew,
Male and female amazingly created by him,
The atmosphere also became new.

We only knew that the sky was higher,
Then Stars embrace galaxy unending distance,
Where destiny began our life and character,
The realm of hope brought new science.

Man and woman created for terrestrial reign,
The painter, the performer's spoken word,
Became breath and soul purchase by design,
And richness in heart dwells in joyful mode.

Sun and evening pursuit comes within a dream,
Night stopping by the woods quietly listens,
Angel's voices the fantasy of pleasure esteem
Oblige the soul in unfortunate misgivings.

Strength transplant to a road of weakness
The embryo of sin our beautiful world entrenched,
The ambiguity of abuse and sadness,
Reconstruct the growth of every living branch.

But we did not suffer total rejection,
Man and woman could not sink any deeper,
Into earth's home they found sauntering companion
And live with love and tolerance for each other.

# Missing pieces in the puzzle

There are dozens of reasons
Apart from the obvious why a lover left you
Missing important piece in the puzzle
The anguish adding up to so many in fact
That really none make sense at all.

Confusion grips your thoughts
Enter connection Promising freedom
And some immediate relief from anguish
Many Questions and comments
Empowered the reason they left

The main reasons why lovers leave
Because they are torn between choice
Hiding important pieces in the puzzle
Some try winning their way back to deceive
Keeping score through all the real trouble

Knowledge can save you from different anguish
Your are not alone, the part they gave you
They had promise others heart and soul
The same thing no one ever had
Important Missing pieces in the puzzle

Real connection missing love and passion
Someone else tried to jump the gun
Making you feel even more special
You appreciate their true intentions
To find the missing pieces in the puzzle

Don't leave one person for another
Expect to be left with only the clothes on your back

If you're lucky make the decision personal
Leave the predator's perspective
Still trying to find the missing pieces in the puzzle

## **<u>My Decision</u>**

When I get to my older self, sunk and shrunken
In the nights of darker days consist,
But I will not go into this contamination
I am strong; I will avoid it at all cost.

I can see a light shining bright in the window,
And it is coming towards where I am sitting.
Maybe what I am seeing is my shadow.
I hate bright lights, the silent image they bring.

Hiding their faces, you can tell they are slow
I am making my decisions but I am trembling
I making will for all my children to know
I am not worried about living or dying.

And Have grown accustom to their silence
Really they don't trouble me, but I am watching,
To see where they go when they leave my presence.
I am here waiting for the angels to come calling.

Although I can't hear a sound, I am not leaving here,
Perhaps it is more beautiful in heaven
I told God I will be late, but I am tried to get up there,
I know my sins have been forgiven.

But I am not in a hurry, when I get there God will begin
Handing out the rewards, crowns and gold pins
For enduring different kinds of pain
And there will be plenty of surprise pilgrims.

# **<u>My Desire</u>**

There stood before me
Is the object of my desire?
Anxiety running through me,
I feel a flame of loving fire.

I see a shadow coming closer
I don't want to be frighten,
But my heart is the prey to desire
And I am the hunter's victim.

Now so close I smell the flavour,
Tearing at my heart into what I want,
To take my fill of this desire,
And I am still been hunted.

I fall into a deadly path of excitement,
Trembling more with fear than fantasy
Standing on the edge of descent,
Set down into a life of reality.

# <u>Never Ending Blessings</u>

There's always that special moment
That brings you back in time,
With nostalgia quaint and faint,
And covet verses come to mind.

Playing sublimely over again,
In a song that you will remember,
And hope the grayling tune
Would not escape into the air.

With individuals names you will hear,
Shinning betwixt memories and stars
They're a never ending blessings
Until heaven blacken the scars.

Fame regaining a new choir,
It wasn't for the things that happened,
In disguise during the last year,
And events we have taken for granted.

There is always going to be the sharp pain,
That is killing you from inside,
And leave you teary eyed stain.
Emotions start with fear and begin to hide.

The confuse flow of poignant feelings,
With voices disguising broken promises,
The heart cries out in voiceless peelings
And that prayer brings you back to your sens

# Obsessions

Perused by persistent images
Of obsessions, the thought takes a deadly form
And reality and fate rearranges,
All the mistakes in a horrifying dream.

Going through the gate, heaven can wait,
I gaze into space, and stay awake
Caught my soul in control of isolation,
Watching every step a minute make.

To take my place and make me surrender,
Become a number alongside the previous owners,
My life is mine, if only I could live a bit longer
With winners and not with losers.

No one should be allowed to take it away,
I can give another part of me freely,
That was given at birth until I reach eternity,
I will stay here on earth and enjoy my liberty.

When is eternity not an obsession with death?
Only God to whom I will surrender,
Death, where is your final breath?
And the sting is the grave that I will enter.

# One Man One Woman

It's not that I am right to pursue the wrong,
Finding laws govern one man with one woman,
Inequalities of being moral society understand,
Not holding a person's sexuality to ransom.

Love no longer use persuasion to change our mind,
Has medium ran out of having anything worth saying
On male dominance or equality of female demand
Is that right the principle for marriage increasing?

Most people want one man for one woman
And everybody else to be nice with no alternatives,
Because the laws are basically easy to understand,
They are black and white with hidden motives.

With every heavy heart mysterious revelation start
Putting well being behind the common good,
Its ashamed truth can never take president,
And show the trail from where creation went.

From the beginning truth was utterly blown
The messiah who had given life into the world
Those Laws and means humanity now sadly disown,
Set aside in combination gone out of control.

It started with noble principle having everything
Ending up as comedy this society could not imagine,
Falling out of fidelity where natural desire began tiring
Breaking into dehumanizing the pleasures given.
Time whipped up more guilt by the aggrieved,
Seeking the justice reserve in expression of opinion,
They are offended because they were abused
And no one was prepared to stand against the crime.

It is in part offending younger men and women
Those indecencies kept quiet by childlike fear,
Grown up and mature having hurt by definition
Justice should make them laugh while others stare.

Looking at truth through bizarre window
People at the top of the chain started off good,
Meddling in this business became poison arrow
Angry hounds lost all morals for which they stood.

# One moment of Paradise

One moment spent inside of paradise,
Will give us the view that is better
Than a thousand years spent in demise
Measured by the things we surrender.

The consummate art and simplicity absorb
Into the spirit of brilliant personality traits,
In wisdom the soul finds a tutelage sort,
With strength in hand we walk on in haste.

Goodness is found waiting in the afternoon,
To pick a bunch of daffodils from my garden,
And spend time in the shade waiting for new moon
Paradise shines its special kind of light from heaven.

One moment of paradise can come inside
Pours out unlimited sources we cannot hide.

# Our Feelings

A lifelong quest inspired by our emotions,
Fascination felt within the heart soul, and body.
It can drive us to the brink of generosity,
In tireless pursuit, or fantasies of endless passions.

Our feelings goes roaming with strong desire,
Enchantments and intrigued radiates from within.
Brings out character and absorb where we begin,
Fills the low voids, and take the roads we share.

Our the best will seems good yet so misgiving,
Feelings constantly flow from emotional sources,
Explore watery paths and many different courses,
Every day; we all have feelings worth sharing.

The sensational power to engage natural responses,
Our feelings surge to surface anywhere on earth,
We were born with this affectionate gift at birth,
Teardrops at first, and then we hear them in songs.

Beating out lyrics the meaning of interpretation,
Poetry with nothing sweeter than unique feelings,
Engrossed in the midst of joy with new meanings
Release from the heart the fear of consternation.

# **<u>Out in the real world</u>**

At nights, my real world exhale in fears
Such as nightmares in reputation smear,
The dreams challenges its precursors,
Some dismiss what is different behaviour.

The alternatives, struggling between worlds
Making fantasy exchange passion to relocate,
Differences among peers anecdote unfolds,
Conflict moved out due to relapse of hate.

Ingenuity pretends to be our best friends,
Lay and wait; In order to take over the world,
The duel of mind and soul unrequited ends,
Feelings reciprocate in views they hold.

Choosing silent syndrome to find useful reality
Out in the real world around every noisy around
We hear only whisper and see shadows going by,
Hear enraged voices mix up in unsavoury sound.

Awaken by shadows full of strange advances,
People have not ventured far out in the real world,
To meet antics of poverty, voyeurs and romances,
Afraid they will never come back after losing control.

# Pain Shall Have No Power

The pain we hate shall have no lasting power,
And weak it will be when we shall see the sane,
Go without dominion into deaths final hour,
Sink into the ground where they will rise again.

Caught up to the stars to have their names regain,
 When new breath is blown upon their dry bones,
Pain shall have no power nor leave the sting of stain,
Lying under wet earth to clean splintered stones.

Where the wind blows a rose will bloom more,
And lift our heads to see the rainbow in heaven,
But your shadow will bring the clouds together,
Spilt colourful bow until the clouds break down.

Faith in God shall give the sinews strength,
And overcome the cries to the distant ears,
Though changing years have split friends by health,
The pain we hate shall be forgotten in tears.

And no more bright daisies made sad by fear,
Strapped to guilt when they love to pray,
The pain we hate shall have no lasting power,
And our brief parting shall only be for a day.

# Praises to God

In perilous path, resilient on the plains of earth,
On the barren turf, where the bleach dust sow,
Iniquity planted with thorns, darkness brought forth,
Only crushed vines withered by the suns glow.

But the meek of earth sing praises within the heart,
Unto God from where blessings come; and praises go,
In celestial glow, with grace and mercy proclaim truth,
Where love blossom and the lilies of joys grow.

Distant sounds hear the sum of drums beat in heaven,
Sky high clouds carry messages coming from the heart,
Anticipating wonderful praises to God the choice given,
From cleansing souls began a journey of new birth.

To live in peace free from guilt, and proclaim harmony,
In tempted causes of life where the tame minds go,
People give praises to God and blessings accompany,
Go where joy resonates and the still waters flow.

And if earth's society tries to keep glad pilgrims bound,
They in the court of praise ascend the rearward light,
From around the globe, to God it shines; head to womb,
And no wound from hell or hound the heel will bite.

For they are victorious in praises and the radiant beam,
Sends the gospel bells ringing across the plains of earth,
Over land and seas, places herald the wondrous gleam,
Brighter than darkness, the light proclaim liberty and truth.

# **<u>Prayer of Thanksgiving</u>**

Here below, when the cold wind blow,
A voice may cry for those many that will die,
I too; shall have company at my elbow,
And the prayer of thanks rises in the sky.

Spirit going over the grass and white cloud,
With the prayer of gratitude endearing essence,
Passing through testing flames to shout aloud,
Near heaven, aromas of thanksgiving grace.

To live in this world just as we should do,
Sharing with others the joy in my soul,
With no crystal moon to distinguish an ego,
Only pursuit of inner peace I want god to behold.

I am in a realm where we mortals are glad,
When we are sad, to fall upon hands and knees,
In thanksgiving prayer we shall reach our God,
Eternity is destining for truth and justice.

You may leave me on these shores in fire,
But I shall live while grace is abounding,
When the banners fan in their final hour,
I will remember a prayer of thanksgiving.
To the alter burn sun of endearing essence,

# Rain must Fall

We marvel at its beauty and brilliance,
It is a priceless phenomenon,
Which defies the imagery of science?
And spread drops in visible spectrum.

The rain must fall with scattered showers,
Upon parch ground dull and indifferent,
Cloudy atmosphere appear out of thin air,
Connecting forecast to our environment.

From a lofty position in the sky,
Rain must fall with millions of tiny droplets,
In liquid form they come floating by,
And envisage sorrows in teardrops.

You will feel the vapour all around you,
Of warm air holding water condensing,
With torrential downpour towering through,
In spring months increasing.

Rain is a relief reunion of earth and land,
A reservoir of paradise to farmers,
It opens heaven's door and falls like sand,
Over all features it covers.

Then turn and vanished again,
As a stranger that had not been there,
Swung back into the crusading wind,
Over somewhere it feels good to appear.

# **<u>Resurrection</u>**

When from sin we were first forgiven,
Asleep at the foot on frosty bed wake,
Look for locks to open the gates of heaven,
And change the sheet we take.

To hastily dress in graceful dignity,
And mortal things upon which are frown,
Lay in silent arbours to bequeath the clay,
Which made the dust our temporary home?

In walking, and talking, soon we'll be taken,
Since we came into the world with nothing,
We inherited sin, but by grace we are given,
And receive hope to make a new beginning.

Although death, subdue for a moments glow,
In resurrection this world will be renew,
And the weak will live; and rise, and grow,
Immortalize with wind and breath and dew.

Like a crusade wrought for a stately crown,
The transformation of life awaits humanity,
In breath that comes from every sound,
Resurrection opens the gates of prophecy.

Upon where earth lies spinning in space,
So high, that covering penance is meekly worn,
To translate the earthly crown for a fuller grace,
In the presence of God joy is happily worn.

# **<u>Return to freedom</u>**

Greed has torn off society sparkling wings,
Freedom fleeing the ugliness resides within,
Why can't society see desperate conditions?
That humanity is muddled up in.
What is so sweet that life is all about sin?
Without faith return to freedom is incomplete,
Right from wrong we even can't explain,
We miss much and cry too late.
With conscience out of life we can tell,
Another person anything that's on our mind,
And know that all nationalities has free will,
Till their inept culture is refine.
From sore throat right down into the soul,
New age wants to free man from his pain,
But I see stain windows continue to control,
Redemption on man the things of sin.
That reverberates and goes deep within;
Many have not changed their heart,
Only changed membership to begin,
Where association left blank space to start.
Freedom waits at every mans gate,
Hopes get closer when a path is bending,
We are possess by the things we hate,
Leave only thoughtful prints blown by the wind.

# <u>Rivers</u>

In dreams we see the magical flight,
Of crystal waves flying free,
To where the glass of waters meet,
Cruise in a dream upon the sea.

Darkness split the billowing floods,
Flung out brooks into mighty rivers,
To wash the steps down the slopes,
Into slippery streams of tributaries.

Rivers of water run down our eyes,
And let fountain disperse into tears,
In search we find the painful wishes,
Define the sum of all our fears.

The rush of tears we cannot control,
Memories enter the draining basin,
Sorrows like rivers meanders in our soul,
Feelings poured into floodplain.

We heard their voices from the deep,
Soul of our soul where we cannot reach,
The cry which leaves the darken void asleep,
In lonely shadow seen on the beach.

Together we stand, amidst the defiant roar,
And souls that lie at ease deep beneath,
Sleep in tragic tombs amidst the surfing water,
And spirits sail on to the safest harbour.

# Roommates

We meet roommates sharing the same space,
With complete strangers a new friendship begin,
Trying hard to hide their moderate taste,
Eating together and barley wearing nothing.

Without whispering insult or villainous speaking,
Roommates overwhelm at first,
Want to know every move the other is making,
To get along and developed a thirst.

Pride gathers the need to make acquaintance,
More questions are ask than answers are given,
Applied wisdom to appease the listening silence,
And avoid heated squabbles haemorrhaging.

Drawn boundaries in relationship communicate,
The privacy of understanding manner,
To change behaviour and get along with a roommate,
Is an achievement of social power?

Respecting the other when friends cannot be found,
And share laughter sprawled out in dorms,
Tensions are driven to grudge the outer bounds,
Leaving roommate reading elementary forms.

# Running for my life

With one foot off the ground,
Then another image split time
Feel every second hearing every sound
Erasing desires from my mind.

The crisp morning clouds
Fly low with each drop of rain packed tight
I am walking through the crowds,
But my soul is having a fight.

Full trail marathon mostly uphill
Wet and aching feet and sore joints
Longing to see finish time and hear final bell,
I fell on slippery roads at turning points.

Watching time reduces the gap
Running through troublesome pain
I'm at peace with each small drop
Never give up going one step at a time.

Age comes to enjoy the fearful silence
In the middle of this earthen treasure
I run in city streets to country distance
Racing with life pack tight with adventure

# **<u>Sacred Gathering</u>**

Shadows swamp the air with a blanket of fog,
Move mythical clouds from under the dark sky,
Fitting the past sleekly within our memory,
Familiar faces buried long ago in the cemetery.

Nimbly stood stones erect as ruin pillar post,
Forgotten names shimmer in glory halls of fame,
A sacred gathering in the future with the past,
Meet history looking for friends to rise again.

Spirits gather quietly to watch at every funeral,
A world created to celebrated charm and wit,
Innumerable company posses the ethereal,
Our heroes walk slowly up into hollowed light.

The rapture of delta forces multiply in the sky,
The just are blessed, resurrected and translated,
Churned by the world martyrs greeted in eternity,
And given the rewards joyfully anticipated.

The tears we shed can make our hearts frail,
But in heaven; there will be a sacred gathering,
That no dusty method of frail flesh can assail,
Till all humanity groan in woes be forgiven.

# Sea of Passion

The Stammer is love
That dares not speak its name
Of warmth romance
Absent repeated re-frame.
From long calls devoid of closer flame
Once the sea of passion was full
Now a stranger voice late home
With excitement vapour dull
The voice Sound hesitantly misplace
Whispering foreign promises of comfort
In twilight enraptured taste,

No quarrel can mend what heaven first send
Lips and eyes confess deeper descend
Cruel betrayal broken dreams dress in preteens
Sparkling truth erupted the spreading fire
Acquainted with your inherited desire
Arousing passions silent watchers
Of other eyes looking through a milky window
Scented Candles Watching the fleeting snow
As it falls Ambush without sound
Air recognisant parachute
Quick to Icy ground

Night surrenders the moon
The days march on
Captured your isolated gloom
The sea of passion reserve for another time
Jobs and hobbies you decline
Stillness hides the funeral pine
Companion to fear and friend to despair
Deep sigh strengthen hearts bewildered cry

Raise the hopes you build and destroy
Emotions broken pieces bow to your knees
Burnt out pledges in prayer
Send angels to Starts another fire
Recalling fond memories falling on each other.

# **<u>Second Chances</u>**

Everything reflect; black and white
Good and bad are in People and places,
Nature drifts in to bring intelligence
Darkness of mind is exposing by the light.

What about second chances faith and science?
All those who had not repented of their sins
Will the individuals get a second chance?
In another world besides this realm.

The value of atonement is a new parchment,
To recover truth where our hearts wanted to go,
We perch edgy as birds do upon a narrow rim,
Lost in demise of time because we were too slow,
When technology is over and the script is written.

Careers are done transform into retirement,
Will mankind be given a second chance?
For all the consequences to make penitent.

Relief to live with choice or be force by iron rod,
Will that is heaven in a different kingdom?
Called Cosmopolitan celestial metropolis.
Govern by one indivisible force of God,
On earth power is bound as in heaven,
Omnipotent divinity replaced by humanism.

Not of flesh those citizens without a dream,
The rule of democracy gone within earth,
Fade into obscurity the measure of austerity.

Our frolicking contribute to destructive play,
Images from the past unveil in the future
A choice we could take on this journey

## **<u>Set your mind at ease</u>**

You hear about holidays that people hate
But rarely of exotic taste to find better fare,
But cheap enough for agents to promote
Such resorts which they advertise with flair.
A visa to start will set your mind at ease.
Most controls need to see your passport,
Wait a little in long queues to get into the air
But when you see the clouds from up there.

You think you are almost down there,
And can feel the landing gear quickly bite,
Into the dust with the wind rushing clear,
As keen concierge are prone to take delight
And provide the right service to a customer,
Looking for a treat to make them feel please,
Gratuitous tips will set their mind at ease.

Immigration experts give advice on legit matters,
The request that you must weigh points inside,
To set your mind at ease with the right answers,
Files in the butterfly in briefcase discreetly hide
Risk your disk accessory to confide passports
The spiced taste of medicine given in health advice,
Hot desert awaiting to match the hazardous pursuit,
Of pleasures snuggled up with more stress and hurt.

# Sharing Life with Love

Life is a sweet melodious rose
From the territory where we are living,
The choice of life we choose
Love is about sharing and giving.

When the world is unforgiving
Nations are born into one blood
We must be strive to live loving
And practice being good.

The rhythm of enchantment
Can hear musical melodious tune,
Swept along the earth's movement
Dispel darkness and gloom.

Little is known apart from a name
Given at birth by strangers
A treasure full of butterfly pain
We grow and live among the dangers.

# <u>Shattered Dreams</u>

Shattering dreams in roaring times
Pierce the air with voices of wanton cries,
Multitude of people in the age of beauty,
Is dawn to the lines of fashion ingenuity?
Intimate clothes, compelling, and adorable,
Every fabric of imagination is possible.
The economy of golden age already tarnished
In failures victory is already conceived.
Although some doubt what we are seeing
Hope shines more elusively in our dream.
From minds poised in graceful brilliance,
The language of linguistic countenance,
We desire to see fulfilment of our dreams
All the emotions dazzling in the streams,
The glittering destiny we were once convince
Had we seen the shadows in prophetic glimpse,
The aquarium world is a realm locked in a cage,
Earths fate dangling amides the forgotten age,
Where beauty began old age is given a crown
To the hoary head lurking with insipid frown.
Condemning the changes of this new society
Our dreams are shattered in mixed community.

# Signature of sunshine day

Hours go by as sunrise greet the day
Bloom bright between dawn and noon
When the evening at last sun turn grey
Sleepers joined the night and the moon.

A body of darkness cured up in the shade
Sleep through the deep waterfall nature install
Light to stretch out from heaven and invade
Earth unwrap the wrinkled cold from the stall.

Inspired sight of wisdom in pursuing heart
Sunshine help the garden flowering vine
The signature of sunshine day burning bright
In aromas fragrance that exist with time.

Sleep and watch until the next daylight
Bloom bright before the gloom
Fold up tight again and carried in the night
Everything signs the signature of our fortune.

# Your Love is simply irresistible

Your love is simply irresistible
All my impulses were awaken,
By the splendour of your smile,
Ambush my heart with captivation.

I surrendered and made my decision,
Your craven desire holding my heart
So sweet were the moments of passion,
I am still caught in the realm of thought.

Your love is a gift; simply irresistible
Giving it all to me with a special kiss,
A life for the future invest little by little
And I see the stars in dreams and bliss.

I watch your smile exude a raw sensuality,
With beautiful possession of thought swirling,
Around in relentless expression of possibility,
Accentuate the feelings I carry within.

You're smothering gaze amaze with raspy joys,
Takes me in your arms and charm before a fall,
Leave me in heaven at the gates of pearl
Feel in the soul the warmth happiness employs.

# Sleep

A weary tide breaks through the realm,
And suspends the mind in recurrent fate,
Distract the conscious state of living being,
To form the rejuvenation slumber creates.

In sudden twitch the hallucination finds,
Light pierce into darker shadows of the mind,
And sleep conserves the energy which defines,
The sensory strength activity suspends.

In awareness of memorable dreams made,
Time elapse into spheres of hypnotize power,
Counting prismatic stars into infinity fade,
Spinning tricks on icy clouds of fire.

With feelings without fear, we go anywhere,
On a journey through the mind; sleeping fine,
Illusions drop down into similar nightmare,
And the powers we possess take us out in time.

To forget the furious under delirious breathe,
Silence draws the slain day into another night,
Right where sleep can walk with death and myth,
And elude the illusive fear to merge into light.

From the hour we awake with eyes deeper in debt,
The water stilled in tears wash dreams from sleep,
And count the hours we go back to the reposeful gift,
Until the counting down stoop in silence to weep.

# <u>Sleeping among the stars</u>

The welcome sting clings on at the end of day
With hearts and hands and concerted stands,
We make the most of the last demands to pay
Inside the scars we wear among the other wounds.

The warm sweat drip down into a lingering line,
Stick to wrinkled brow define upon the fretted face,
Through the deep fog sleep enters the murky mind,
Feeling aching restrain the heart must embrace.

Fatigue has inspired the mind to cast a snaring web
And trap future moments in the cage where we wait,
Then change the posture into shapes upon the bed
We find resting place under blanket until we are late.

Sleeping among the stars mingle in a fondant dream,
Refuge lay discreet guarded by the intrigue spirits
Shirk when we awake by revelation we have seen,
Gentle warmth we feel in the company of angels.

In whatever shade dreams came by luck or by chance
At the entrance of day to drip down into our soul,
And wait among the stars in amaze to fall and dance
We wear our hearts in a trance that melts with gold.

# Snowballs

I began to live a playful dream,
With the first snow fall,
Of dusty white flakes gathered clean
To throw snowballs
At my friends,

And filled their mattered hair,
Body and flush face,
With pleasure and snowy laughter,
In smiles running down their face,
Hiding the hint of crispy ice,
Rolling down the neck,

I pick the snow up in my hands,
To become a powder ball on its way,
To my friends cheeks,
Flung with fun in play,
Water and ice melting in flight,

Display the magic of the atmosphere,
Rolled into a wand,
Throwing snowballs in the air,
Age has little to do with the fun,
Of throwing snowballs,
While friends try to hide and run

# **<u>Sonnet about Control</u>**

When I was young, hearing the great voice of dad and mum
Exactly what the procedures was I could not understand,
Measures at home, filling the void their parents had begun
Key prevention dominates the room and captured command.
The value of control fanning their idolize way of domination
How to exercise caution through the experiment of authority,
We became strong, took ownership and demand
determination
The things we love and hate took notions in our community.
The bad go wandering might benefit from regulate adventure,
The good procedures parting checks that needs new direction,
Waves of high standards surrender the framework structure
In struggling man lies the curb of undefeated milestone.
Quantum of awards shape the chains that keep them bound
Controlling decades evoke powers with discipline sound.


# **<u>Sonnet about tap dancing</u>**

An airy tune plays flavours we adore
Generate the breathe of vibrant sound,
Tap politely crescendo shoes on the floor
Dance stance move lightly off the ground.

Into this movement of swing and speed,
Trapped charm in space by metallic plates,
The choreography steps and style succeed,
To shuffle the dances combination creates.

Unique blend for either student or enjoyment

Evoke rhythm flames with creative elements
Known and shown where originality meant,
Entertainment display enthuse the movements.

By arts the intent of skill is given for learning,
Magical poetry found in the thrill of dancing.


## **Sonnets**


The loss of memory is forgotten in the wind
The moment we die before our breathe falter,
We are a fading Spectator struggling to the end,
And life flushes out the things we cannot alter.
Stand to surrender and wave the battered flag,
On chosen fields of love serenade career misery,
Some battles we win, but in others wearily drag,
Our soul from the ground to win unlikely victory.
Taste the peace in whose arms we are thrown,
The lifeline we find a sonnet of solace to climb,
Happier days of virtue spent recovering at home,
Leave the cares and thoughts for others to find.
Adventurous world resign from gaining riches,
Embrace sonnets sense of peace and happiness.

# <u>Sonnets about Breakfast</u>

After night manna entwined the morning
We awake to the finest sound of language,
Continental breakfast is the first meal taken,
Bridge the gap between hunger and courage.

People sitting around breakfast bars and tables
Splendid spoonful eaten until almost lunch,
Exchange old kinds of deepening values and fables
Bat cannot changing the way we live in a rush.

Even cereal portions are profoundly healthy,
At the first dawning, the lunchtime that strives,
Arrives before dinner and rush hour bring kindly
Mingled workers homeward from different offices.

Night clears away the dark for breakfast bite,
Stoves and trays lay out amenities to tempt appetite.

# Sprain with pain

From heavenly realm he came to reign,
A lone volunteer stain with pain for everyone,
His days were short within the global frame,
He made the sick well and gave them new vision.

Flushes out the pain stained against humanity
The indispensable contribution highly esteem,
We have not seen all the suffering of society
But sacrifice for good of mankind was given.

By the crimson blood that in time led the crowd,
And paid the penalty for all who may never know
How deep the debt he went for the greater good
Shows the demonstration of love bestow.

Strength and wisdom gives a standing ovation,
We must grow stronger in understanding this power,
Hope will call us away within a glorious selection,
Find a neutral place for us all be together.

# State of Mind

Experience of state makes the flow great
Much more entertain than physical training,
A mental state formation the mind exert,
Endurance emerges of positive thinking.

State of mind running mostly with aching pain
It's at the end you will drop into a small heap
Adulation creates before the medals are reaping.
Enjoy the warrior sprint that ends with a limp.

Time flows in realms of psychological stream
Mental state of mind takes away real happiness
Experience the flow going fast into physical gain
Lose the world immersed into self awareness.

Leaving the dirt, leaving the strain and waste
A mass exodus outside the state of finding a dream
Recovered from the state of people being diagnose
Lost in a world digging for the hope they had seen.

Delusions on the track reflect back to childhood,
Age raise the state of incredible phenomenon
Slipping in and out of time where the world stood
Detached from outside and lose all interest of them.

# Still Waiting

Every sixty seconds spent waiting,
On the reality to obtain promises,
Could be a minute of inheritance gone?
Never to come back and take chances.

More time may elapse after still waiting,
And you may grow faint and weary,
But preserved confidence in expecting,
Fulfilment of promise to make you happy.

Keep waiting to inherit the promises,
For this is what patience implied,
If we believe, faith preserves appearances,
To see the glory for which others has died.

Sitting awake in the dark still waiting,
Being who I am claiming to be,
The solitude of memory is everything,
A secret at the time belong in me.

On a trail where mystery is what I am doing here,
As if watching silent glimpse of myself,
The waiting goes on around the next corner,
Always passing the enterprises I felt.

# **<u>Sugar Cane</u>**

This year the crop is perfectly sweet,
Sugar cane hanging lollipops in the fields,
Where tropical sun bends the harvest into it,
Propped up by a line as blustery trees;
Produce more sugar cane than I have ever seen.
The taste is sweet, but no farmer has
Chosen this variety of intoxication merit,
A thing of beauty just to look on it;
The juice is rung to put in your mouth,
And chew the flavour till all flakes are crush,
In joyful moves, sugar meddles with the tongue,
Along the labyrinth of our catching apatite.
We chew it strong before press into rum,
And the taste of another kind together crossed
Our mind, when the strength that is young,
Merge the creation of two greater spirits,
Strong teeth in the mouth can enjoy the harmony.
Sugar cane, the flavour begins sweet, and never ends,
Where the folly of the world rends; flesh craves
The passion with strong drink rages.
The woes lick the wounds and suck lollipop strength,
To draw the first blood, in social light,
And darkness sees light when night is nearly done,
The moon goes all the way up to space,
Then earth gains back the seed it had sprung,
Turn hot sugar cane to grow tall in the grass,
Yearly spun nature maturing rain and sun,
Life is dependent on harvest in the fields;
People can start to prepare for another dream.

# <u>Sushi</u>

Love not too much by many,
Edible flavour found in Sushi,
Press into ball shape Varity,
Smelled raw like the sea.

Etiquette cuisine as distinct as nature,
We look away leaning across the table,
And see scattered rice and Nora,
Lay bare and feeble.

We are very tired when we are hungry,
Many fingers to this palate would drop,
Eating Sushi rolls to make merry,
Even if given bucketful of gold.

Rather eat an apple or a pear,
Than fermented fish evolved as it descend,
From the mouth to later appear,
Where the wind comes cold.

Wash with the morning vapour,
Separate thoughts wept and crept,
To ease the accentuated flavour,
Wrapped floundering in secret.

# **<u>Tears from Heaven</u>**

When there is nothing more say,
Tears say goodbye to our heaven,
And leave the shadow of today,
Sink into darker images exploding.

The tragic prize of a broken heart,
Sends messages through the air,
When everything has fallen apart,
Tears engage the waiting atmosphere.

And haunt the staring eyes,
Foamed in fire and feelings,
To make the skin shiver with fears,
As tears fall they crush everything.

Yet Inside opportunity demands,
More inseparable chiming of sequence,
Finds the attraction of emotions,
A hurtful truth brush with chance.

Crush in the parade on fading view,
Tears stimulate angels in heaven,
They see the hurt and come to our rescue,
A guardian when we need a friend.

# That Hidden Desire

I lost that hidden desire
The things I once possess,
I think I lost the blazing fire,
Dreaming of them becomes obsess.

Is life worth living?
When you lose the will to live
Work all your life labouring
Trying to give and forgive.

I am trying to recover
You can see that I have nothing,
No money hidden, only the will power,
Seeing that I have nothing.

You could try and help me,
Find myself doing something,
To help others trying to be,
What their soul want desiring.

Everything is worth nothing
Unless you become better person,
Seeing that you have nothing,
Living to give of yourself a reason.

Secret can no longer hide the changing
When you're getting old,
It's worth desiring to sacrifice everything
To save a single lost soul.

# The Boys inside

They come back almost losing shirt and shoe,
Breathe glow in flames of sports and laughter,
When it is still too hot to tell mother a joke or two,
They delight themselves in their usual manner.

The boys inside are locked up, live out their fears
In childhood days have more frequent dreams to hide,
The tears rein the stain that will grimly bear their fears
Illuminations from outside thrills the little lad inside.

A survivor or saviour, future glare where freedom share
Far flung fun optimism in different stages of the age,
Some tall and thin, others huggable bears free with flair
Encapsulates all the treasures found on earthly stage.

Giving courage in brutal weather deny soul and body
Live to tell the story again and take every chance they get
Never to surrender the sword of words clutch neatly
In heart, soul and mind, and all the learned intellect.

# The Broken Mirror

Most ambition starts with a dream,
And never ends when the night brings,
A wicked thought in a natural stream,
Fantasy is not seen when the alarm bell rings.

The chimes of reality try to awake you,
But you are lost where pain can't be seen,
And correction is too hard for heart to renew,
Everyone you thought was so highly esteem.

Some wore terror, others brought boredom,
Come to use you for another adventure,
Duplicity is a two edge sword of persecution,
And carries a frown reflected in the mirror.

We can always find time to laugh or weep,
Bliss, marriage, occupation appear discreet,
When the pieces are broken they cut deep,
And the mourners go about the street.

A house of mirrors has broken cracks,
They widen and will not procrastinate forever,
Before shattering into small magic pieces,
And the original beauty is lost forever.

# The days have passed

The days have passed won and lost,
In a gesture copied to whatever love takes,
And memories wait to be quietly rescued,
From a lifetime of irreconcilable urges.

A worn vow parted from my heart,
And rolled into a tighter clasp,
To bind my soul still against the dying light,
Bruised with fierce tears I cannot gasp.

Perfect deeds within the obituaries,
Are as grief flown away on wings to the future,
Parting from the past like crystallite meteors,
Caught our memories and sank the waning fear.

The days have passed your home at last,
But we will always have the happy hours,
And carry each other's secret at all cost,
In the wind and shadow that passes.

And sailed towards the isles that wait for me,
In beauty sleep the days have passed,
And the night is fast approaching eternity,
To where new life will conquer, win and lost.

# The Feeling of Love

Your touching lips is the scarlet line touching mine
Glows in the moonlight and reborn each morning
Delivers the feelings which brings warmth into mind
Then on earth, gives the pain of love departing.

When the moment pass away to inherit new furls,
Foul dust floated on the ragged edge of the universe,
Where mystery unfolds feeling of personality hurls,
Life hidden place between our dreams and chosen choice.

The feeling of love goes sobbing into holes of stone,
Once wet and swollen, now dry and standing afar,
As if everything that existed before had merged into one,
And cut so far to leave the bereaved in need of care.

Feelings cry from within but they are not alone,
Here we build bridges and crosses of our own.

# The good will prevail

We find grace and mercy
Truth and compatibility
We were meant to share,
The dreams we treasure.

And so in your arms
Among in choice charms
The darkness I do not fear,
The doom cannot compare.

When your name is spoken
My heart is quickly awoken
Love hides the dark in your light
Your love is pure and bright

While others may promise,
The wealth of riches
They fade and then fail
But the good will prevail.

# The Great Consolation

Jesus was moved to tears at the grave of Lazarus
He experience the agony the family felt
He remembered their loss
He was their great consolation
Into a dark tomb went the light
And looked with compassion upon his children
Their sorrows touched his heart
Jesus wept aloud and could have cried more
His human nature could not escape pain
Their pain he knew by the tears he was willing to share
And he gave to their troubled hearts the light of hope
He turns the darkness of death into a new dawn
Gave them strength to cope
And a more glorious light await
The sorrow of parting into the joy of heaven
They will meet again by the eternal gate
When the saints go marching in

# <u>The Hurricane Breathe</u>

Melancholy cloud lining the sky
With storm showers crying out loud,
The heavenly grief is a weepy canopy,
Shelter foggy dust when thunder is heard.

The passing breeze is earning its keep
Plunder the atmosphere sowing death,
A casket of misfortune in the harvest it reap,
From the hurricane melancholy breathe.

They burst their banks and the sea rises
Creeping unveil fast upon the land,
From the bottomless pit the rain disguises,
And the hurricane march strong upon the sand.

In the lap of nature birth strong winds
Leaving the sand fade back into dense rim,
Water that mighty hurricane sends,
Holds earth in the palm of its hand.

The duration catches people unprepared,
Trees and house falls into disrepair,
The passing breeze of danger we all feared,
Came and took our plans into deeper despair.

# <u>The New Age</u>

Beyond this present strand,
Herald the dawn of a new age,
With another incomplete generation,
And we leave the past to go on pilgrimage.

People reaching out for a new start,
Fleeing the present awful destiny,
With the shame and guilt of our past,
Crossing the rippling tides of history.

New heritage to explore a beautiful concept,
Leaving the dark dusty spirit,
Of this fading world dying debt,
With guilty pleasures we must neglect.

There is doubt in every candidates vote,
Stumbling on with promise accountability,
History rewritten on a new bank note,
And each decision causes more anxiety.

The new age owes no maintenance,
Over the darkness of this generation,
But offers hope and a life more intense,
Than the existence of present cohesion.

I will watch as new horizon turn the page,
Bands play music for the decade to dance,
We wait patiently at the crossing of a new age,
The decision of faith spun by chance.

New age may bring hope and credibility
But only where things exist of simplest nature,
To brighten the future with our destiny,
In pursuit of many more hopeful desire.

# The Poor Is Wealthy

Blessings upon them conceived,
And the rich becomes empty,
By the root of evil they are deceived.

The humble rejoice,
Knowing life in the balance
Prayers are answered with grace,
Gods will in our conscience.

Whatever you magnify,
Will become your god,
The poor is wealthy,
Sometimes they are sad.

When their eyes are wet,
Like blur violet, it's hard to be proud
Feeling totally inadequate,
The poor put their trust in God.

Blessed are the poor in spirit;
For theirs is the kingdom of heaven.
Those who recognize they have no credit
There is treasure stored up for them.

Some are rich and have acquired wealth,
God chosen those who are poor,
In the eyes of the world to be rich in faith,
And inherit a kingdom on the celestial shore.

# The Rapture

I will be in heaven, where there are no more torments,
School holidays slips away in tears, winter wakes cold
Brush the gloom away with longer disappointments
The doom of unbelievers hastens to wrap itself in self pity
All the righteous mantle bring their faith close to God
Mankind stands in the gap looking out into eternity
Then come the new revelation, who are the worshippers,
Bound for the marriage supper in heaven angels awaiting
The rapture hovering round the church alter to pray,
Swift will come that day, trumpets blow the gutsy sound
And all the saints suddenly dash to meet the lord in the air,
This race is will call saints from around the entire world
To the gathering in the sky they will come
Men of old, women untold, children and friends
The fastest wind takes them quickly into the sun,
Fly with eagles to a brighter day.

# The Revolution of our Personality

Why do you need to change personality?
When so many things are already addicted to yourself,
New discovery of lifestyle health and beauty,
Can be found in our world where we are seeking wealth.

You're probably going to leave the old force of nature,
To pursue a new realization in a fabulous discovery,
But there is more to stylish images than a glossy picture,
Virtue wears the changes in our unique personality.

Within the human heart experience the connecting taste,
There is something more born from deep appreciation,
We make a new start without the time we waste,
Making therapeutic explanations for our emotion.
In the heart is where personality revolutionizes,
Pick us up with new feelings when we are down,
Provides exactly what we want to see regenerated our lives,
Namely the dreams we experience on our own.
Then comes hope wherever we are place in the world,
Rare jewels of splendour dresses the mind of humanity,
And personalized all the different choices we may hold,
Life is based not on fashion alone but on our personality.
These are high stakes we assuredly are able to find,
Such profile for the present time is a rare commodity,
The unique claim is perfect but we are marred with time,
Probably leave dreams wandering about our personality.

# The Root of My Convictions

Life begins many causes uncertain
But in faith start to draw the curtain,
And expose the root of my conviction,
Suspend the evidence on probation.
To relieve me of the threat in my head,
I am force to take up reasoning instead.
Rejected by friends by harsh tempest
I Pay the debt owe to society doing my best.
With better morality comes painful urge,
Wandering in blur visions looking to purge,
Deeds swept away from wise dry eyes,
Learning to control nightmares and tears,
Bound to live while there is still a little time
With exchange heart and changes in mind,
Only memories bring the partial plague,
Procreate events of danger and intrigue.
The secret lodge betwixt my old soul,
Light the rusty fuses that was dull.
And in my heart turn on the ignition,
Its direct powers root out my conviction.
Delayed success shall run rampant
In making priorities more important,
Embrace the dreams of last opportunity
Take pleasure now in things of beauty.
Than the misfortune first encountered
The things that charmed me most has halted
The flame runs unhindered through my head,
They will lay my soul asleep upon my dying bed.

# The Sanctuary within

The whisper of breeze on my face,
Send confidence to the sanctuary within,
Oozing pain coming without trace,
The agony spilled out with delirious scream.

Hope brings out a triumphant joy,
Resonate from the sanctuary within,
Prayers to heaven send the call of victory,
And the greatest prize we are about to win.

Winners; we shall be not be deceive,
With ease of wearing Olympic crowns,
Fear not the trigger nor do the taunts conceive,
The flint that makes pride takes you to dreams.

If my doubts had not vanished away,
I would have reclined and fainted with unbelief,
But on my way I went into the sanctuary,
And look for the fortune of hidden relief.
Infinity of modern voices, the crowd rises,
The globe attraction of tremendous attention,
Adrenaline wrapped in present applauses,
The emotions began dilating within.
I had fainted in the land of the living,
Overwhelm by celebration of winners,
Clutching the torch of existing flame,
That exhibit gold and silver names.

# The Scent of summer

The woodpecker picking skins from the trees,
Summer air hardly blowing, heavy and humid,
Make female flutter in the wind as naked goddess,
Greet the fluttering fan blowing in their hand.

A windy ripple of joy amides fragrant the smiles,
Like the scent of mist loitering in a new morning ray?
Falling from heaven upon rugged hills with limpid tress,
Make a noise blushing in leafy shade of the day.

Up in the sky, morning glory shows a brilliant fire,
And the young hairy grass whisper with a different voice,
Call unto drowsy fields for nature to awake from slumber,
Take into the air beauty of presiding choice.

Between dimpled leaves come the buzzing bees,
Clouds go higher, gathered sweat in boughs as rain,
The season bring the scent of summer bloom with ease,
Mingled fragrance in the lovely leaves contain.

A special display of all the aspirations that people have,
Stored up in many small changes of fresh fantasies,
Orchards paths in distant dreams many do crave,
But we can all swallow reality much nearer the pansies.

In sunset shadows the glitter of gold pass sublimed,
Where painted mausoleum pervades dark places,
Which mark that imprint in the sands of our time?
Wind and rain gently step aside from the gorgeous isles.

# **The Strong Man**

The Bible tells us about a man, who became strong,
He was ruled by rage and lived in a foreign land
He was big and tall and builds like the city wall
And declared that no one could make him fall.
He had long spears and sharp knives,
They called him uncircumcised hated and despise,
He brag about his powers and his enemies fate,
But he too would not have long to wait.
Before meeting a young soldier practicing his faith,
An invisible kingdom provided his strength,
He was not big and tall but had a powerful guard,
And declared his faith in the true and living God.
Out of the two men the latter was the strongest,
Not for his muscular brawn but for the help request,
He became the stronger man restoring a nation's pride,
When brave men sought a place of refuge to hide.
His trust in God was scorned and mocked,
But suddenly all their mocking would stopped,
Slain by the might of heavenly force in full flight,
And his enemies scattered to hide their fright.

# <u>The Unchanging Spirit</u>

The unchanging spirit
Comes from the beginning
Grant the life we inherit
Can also change our destiny,

And gives hope to all for eternity,
We can take the convictions,
As a unique offer of security,
Or look for other reasons.

Even pretend to pass it on
For someone else to deal with,
Deny the conviction of solution,
And try to breathe a sigh of relief.

In another moments breath
Life could simply be over
Lose wealth gone in poor health
Our prayers God will answer.

Given by the unchanging spirit
He has a great deal of blessings
Waiting in heaven for us to take,
We can shout about many things.

God promises the assurance
Of blessings upon our lives
When we mess up there is grace,
In deliverance the Spirit gives.

# The world is turn upside down

The search begins on land and then to the moon,
Charmed into wild storms of fatigue and intrigue,
While loneliness invades the world with gloom,
Earth weeps in the upheaval it has sown with grief.

God guides words design to chasten our hearts,
Come free from heaven the showers we need,
Wash clean on seraphs wings the guardians imparts,
Defeat in parts only, some strong demons concede.

The world is torn in upheaval by good and evil
Trying to be the masters, but who wins the prizes?
We are caught between realms as a travelling vehicle
People are torn between the choices of lovers.

The fabric fraying; decadent society falling for magic
Looking for clues into space observing all the planets
Turn broke countries upside down for another trick,
Not seeing the rift of relationship in the continents.

Hate loiter where grace and mercy was meant to share,
On this demise terrain fear no alien with foreign gold,
The enemy is our love gone cold, and feels insecure,
Paradise lost opposite paradox world.

Search betwixt disasters for new strength to cope,
Few sweet melodies rise from the life we are living,
Destiny Answers the call of many souls seeking hope,
Sharing and giving where emptiness is unforgiving.

# <u>This Is Like Heaven to Me</u>

Heaven is where we walk the streets made of gold,
And secrets of our hearts will be told.
The further we go the heavenly sunset we behold
Thinking of heaven where angles are ordained of God
Around the throne eternity is bound,
Wound in celestial mantle our old prayers are found.

Where you will never age, and see sunrise in the dark,
Waiting for the star and the dewy morning light,
Appearing so bright the night is soon forgotten.
Heaven wakes the stations in the entire kingdom,
A new enchantment waiting to be discovered,
A secret world lies between heaven and earth.

Walking daytime if you are immortal full of life,
On earth life is hell; our lives are like empty shell.
We carry misery from early birth to the deep earth,
Belief keeps us looking for heaven in the clouds,
In hope of humane rapture that will give peace.

And take in the dim view; to a place that is new
Where teenagers can dress like linen lilies.
Hiding a sermon you cannot walk to church with,
The sign makes the heart free from the pain of fear.
And the sky above them are laden with smoke,
Dreams which could be paradise move uneasy,
The next day life is different when they awake.

This is like heaven to me with love and dreams,
I will wait patiently until my destiny come.
They see the blue skies above and watch the smoke
Move gently through the clouds away from the crowd,
Gathering storm brings the rain that will quickly fall,

One of Gods messenger touches the Glover grass.
And soon the dark shadows past into the night,
Be reborn in the harvest of heavenly paradise.

On the street where I live there is a ladder to climb
Tall hedges and scented foliage blind the golden sun,
That sweet savour with leaves fluttering in the wind,
Turned the pages as they move below the window pane,
They seemed too changed and turn a different colour.

And the heart looses gain and falls apart with pain,
The realm of this world tries to take control,
Angels tells a different story running from heaven.
My mind does not exist among the clouds
When the rain falls, blessings feel like I am forgiven

African violet sometimes your eyes are wet,
But the showers needs to fall on barren hearts,
Places we have been and the things we regret.

# <u>This is Paradise</u>

Geography tells us about a beautiful island
Invention by wood and water in the Caribbean,
Upon this sunny terrain pleasures stands tall,
And opens the gate of paradise to entertain all.
See the glow in the sky when the sun bends low,
And dipped stunning view into the blue sea below,
Distinction washes white sands upon wishing shores,
Where we lay engage in rows of intrinsic paradise.
Those who come take their turn for different choices,
With this in mind; the preoccupation of tropical paradise
Many try to find a key to adopt this kind of lifestyle,
But it will take a greater sum to bring out a perfect smile.
For this island is paradise waiting to be discovered,
A kingdom where uncovered dreams are gathered,
To explore the shifting brilliance fanaticism in a trance,
Embrace the accolades which we will always reminisce.
Flashes advance the myth but never quiet lift off the cliffs,
West End becomes the place where excitement drifts,
All carnal things the spirituals scorned and mocked,
Suddenly they are the main attractions to reach the top.
From this island a new name will reach other distant lands,
And mark the silken silhouette with all kind s of depths.
Of sunset floating streams with ruses to find and spend,
On self absorbed insight values of the perceptive mind.
For on this island paradise is the dwelling place of heaven,
This kingdom come down upon earth gave gifts to men,
When opportunity clears the path the mystic hope is waiting,
Along will come the rapture and leave bodies still sun
tanning.

# To be Loved

Two women comes into my life
I am sorry I cannot love both,
And be one lover without causing strife
For the way I take leads to truth.

To love and be loved as far as I could,
Love one and leave the other in pain
To stain my name in long ages stood,
Perhaps heaven will have a better claim.

And look down with justice just as fair
To where moral emotions unequally lay,
Though unfair for those passing there,
Not knowing the dangers along the way.

For if they should gamely come back
And find love I doubt it will be the same
Worn path with pain they would walk,
And find steps of reward treading to heaven.

With a smile kept first before they cry,
For a long time they will remember the frown
And shall tell the Intel story with a sigh
On the same path they had previously worn.

For on earth one woman is enough to love
The other realm by heaven to be loved,
And let emotions make a different move
Into the place where truth stood.

# To Be Remembered

When the lord takes me away,
And I am no longer with you,
To share the pleasures of today,
Remember I will always be with you.

When my footsteps can't be trace,
Let my spirit in flight go free,
To find its own precious place,
For the soul to unites with destiny.

And leave a testimony to witness,
In the presence of those still alive,
To be remembered always,
For the living treasures God gave.

Are to be shared among the people,
And to be swept up in ashes and dust,
Till time consume every evil,
And we are gathered to him at last.

# To someone special

Every road we walk upon has a turning point,
Taken by most to find someone special,
From children to parent, we're all different,
God has made one blood of streams without equal.

To another person, we fill the heart with bliss,
By our personality, our character, and intrigue,
And no one else has your art of creativeness,
And if dreams come true, your unique point of view.

To tell the thrill of passion to someone special,
For those wonderful times spent together,
To miss them when you're awake, and stumble,
Quietly to find they were the best times share.

With what matters most, your touch and your smile,
Nobody else is like you, if friend or foe could realize,
You paint a lovely picture of someone special
They will embrace your attributes and ideas.

# Too Far to Turn Back

I have gone too far to turn back from loving you
The pains endured, faith been knock around a little bit,
Committed to virtue, the prize of seeing things through
I have never done before, but my soul refuses to quit.

The most amazing thing is the miracle we are given,
To be born from the most unlikely background,
And be not influence by the bad persons or alien feign
Going on in society, and the environment surround.

But you are not too far behind to get ahead,
Don't allow negative circumstances to dictate fear
It will stop you from growing, keep striving instead
Look for goals in your life and blessings to share.

Life can be cruel; I have come too far to turn back,
Having endured hostile abuse and persecution
From mine adversaries, even friend's vicious attack,
Shame is responsible for the greater proportion.

If you should let faith slips who will take the blame?
Roll with the pain; don't drift away out in the cold
And sell out your soul for picketing of a noble name,
Where would you find comfort as anchor for my soul?

Even thought I am slowing down with age
My career is accelerating towards the finish,
With agility, the rapture assures me of a heritage,
Beyond this sphere lies a greater destiny to reach.

# Touch Others with Tears

When trials descends upon the home,
I am left alone to find solution,
With tears making sheltering atone.

They turned to water and wet my face,
Problems trace the air in silence,
They leave to go and return in haste.

The friends I ask for help,
It seems they too have long slip,
From the positions they had grip.

Their hearts are made of stone,
With passion surrendering decision
I wrestle with passion.

Struggle on trying to understand,
We have to the face trials in our mind,
Treat then as an enemy or a friend.

Realise everything is just for a little while,
We can walk away or even run a mile,
But a problem share though a smile.

Will overcome the winds that blow,
The pain where the tears flows,
Reaching heights of sorrows.

Outside when the tears dried,
Pain goes where tears cannot hide,
The breath we take torment inside.

From the moment you touch others,
See the world through their watery eyes,
Piercing inside with winter tears.


# <u>Tragic Past</u>


Tempted and tried you want to follow,
The things that everyone does.
But you are plague with sorrow,
Of your tragic past comes and goes.

But that's only because you keep reflecting
On the tragic past that binds your heart,
While the pain in process is ripping
Your hopes and your dreams apart.

Many have tried to counsel you but failed
They have tried in vain to ease all the suffering,
From which all the agonies bewailed
And becomes the lament of time.

You ask God to remove this burden.
And give you peace from the life you are living.

# **Troubled Times**

In trouble times there is transformation of suffering,
They please us not the solemn trauma of stress,
It doesn't need to have control if the soul is strong,
You can handle the cure when humanity confesses.

More years are spent in weariness and woes,
Fewer days defy the things our soul merely endure,
They brought human toil early and leave the sorrows,
Some things we hate are not the answers we desire.

We want to rest our minds in green meadows,
With strength to guide when frail spirit grow weak,
Victory to the brave; so bring me comforts in my troubles,
And I will not fear the crumbling earthquake.

Even when I walk the salient way through the valley of death,
The priestly dew of heaven brings the mourning into joy,
I am sure when I pray strength takes all my leaping breath,
And the troubles endure make the sacrifice a greater glory.

Although with grief within we are crush; we are not broken,
Each burden bare well; are the tokens of great deliverance,
Fewer misery spell Immeasurable values to our bodies given,
A kind relief recompense of perfect inheritance.

# <u>Twilight</u>

My heart was racing towards the sunset,
Which stood with misty colours like rainbow?
Painting a poster of people walking straight,
Along the canal in a melancholy row.
To this enchantment I became reminiscent,
Serenading love in the gloomy moments of twilight,
Reality came amidst the youthful testament,
To stir my heart with pleasure and delight.
Engaging dreams reflecting the twilight,
The truth about emotion almost touched oblivion,
Whiles caught in a net by the estranged light;
I toiled hard to find comprehension.
And found familiar joy upon a gondola ride,
Parting waves stripping like pieces of rags,
Roaming along the glassy water path we glide,
Time share recluses and recurrent laughs.

Fading light took disguises under red sky reset,
Reflection release pain into the sea of memory,
Closing the day walled up inside the sunset,
And found no place to hide and shelter reality.
Relief mopped the creasing of my brow,
Until within the flickering path night cross,
The watery snow to find the eternal vow,
Retreating with the atoning kisses.

# Under Attack

I watched and listen well
I came under the relentless attack
Some offenders I knew, others I could not tell
Enemies aim the arrows at my back.

The chain of pain all the emotions start
Voices repel the state of inbred thoughts
Dislikes hides the poison claws in the heart
We hear only the faint whispers of certain parts.

Unpleasant attack made the days full of trouble
Life in particular is made up of evil and good
Who would have thought such things were possible
Seeing the enactment where you stood.

Under attack, life looks empty and bleak
Fear haunts every move you make
Nightmares in dreams make things creak
Into darkness each day the heart will awake.

The friends you once cherish are not so real,
They becomes the enemy in the gate,
With planed mischief mostly how to make you fall
They rise early when you think they are late.

# <u>Upon The Side Walk</u>

Vehicles old and new parked upon the side walk
Here too some people unite while others stare,
With worried looks of doom around them stark
Shedding tears of regret in showers of the heart
Like raindrops falling from heaven
Upon their heads disguise in the clouds
They seek to be forgiven of their imperfection
Staring out into space, yet they don't know why
God made them all meet upon the sidewalk
With good intention progress was not enough,
They smile and try to make small talk
But something is missing from all their stories
The life that can drive a person crazy,
People come to England bearing their soul
They had met many travellers on another road
Come in from the cold and join the fold.

# <u>Voices of the Heart</u>

A shadow far away coming nearer each moment,
With foregone enchantment swifter than light,
The voices of my heart pierce the shadow of night,
Eyes could not have seen the cries made of fright.

Mute stranger not hearing the shuffling prance,
Swayed in dance from the gripping hold of agony,
I did what no opportunity would have given chance,
Pass hastily with prayer into the realm of misery.

My naked soul made the call of hopeful choice,
To try and stem the tide of emotions from inside,
On the floor I went, to end the screams in silence,
And pluck up courage where shame tries to hide.

The bruises appear delirious with implacable scar,
Beyond the soul stronger voices torment the heart,
With imagery pasteurizing the greyscales of fear,
Crying for help, crippled by the passions once felt.

Woken from a dream to the glow of another rising sun,
Visions not forgotten rode by on a brighten screen,
Blearily pursue the papal breath broken and undone,
Were these voices of my heart or a voice from heaven?

In me all the hurt is repeated without honour,
And nothing is forgotten without leaving pain,
To feel the cold chill pass upon destiny€™s shore,
Hearing voices of the heart quietly lamenting.

They had pierce safe barriers and brought cute hell,
Far more darker than the torment life has given,
Repeated voices that arise from my heart to tell,

The story memories would rather have forgotten.

# <u>Waiting For Life to Begin</u>

In the beginning we never knew teardrops,
We were the fashion becoming new,
God's creation brought the raindrops,
And the sky in heaven turned blue.

We only knew the innocence of gender,
Stretched far back into unbending distance,
Beginning our characteristics and behaviour,
The experiment brought new science.

Paused in the realm; waiting for life to begin,
Something's in weakness can be strength,
The embryo of transplant intent stood waiting,
To oblige in the steps of unknown spirit.

Jagged thoughts in age more entrenched,
But hopes springs the proposing grace,
Begin the twist of nature on a bizarre road,
With new creation of continuous race.

Cold calculated chaos began misgiving,
In the beginning opulence was lost,
Temptation found refuge surrendering,
To the existence of a pertinent cost.

Creation suffer rejection and abuse,
And took a ride in ungainly pursuit,
To reconstruct the skills once refuse,
But could not make earth a safer retreat.

# Waiting for something to happen

I have waited before and nothing happened,
This time I am expecting something to happen,
The occurrence may take longer than planned,
Dreams were born in appearance that will begin.

Every part of me left hanging upside down,
Cursing the veil event which had torn apart,
The bliss life known, planned and waiting,
But love says it should have broken my heart.

Bury my head and flush the feelings all away,
Instead, I can start mounting another challenge,
Choosing time and place being suited in array,
Escape that world and be taken by a carriage.

It could be the angelic flight of love from above,
With contented joy embrace the tighten alter grip,
And all the leftovers of my body solemnly move,
Sentiments fashion every thought and tentative step.

I waited for love to paint over the part of my life,
Remove the gloomy birth from all disappointment,
That brought the indolent moods to sense its peak,
And commune with patience the waiting moment.

This could be the dream I have been waiting for,
Anticipating something beautiful in life to happen,
And my passive resistance which stood unsure,
Held a door open until the dream prefer comes in.

# <u>Walk With My Spirit</u>

In a hotel room watching the white snow fall
Glistening past with beckoning mossy leaves,
Drape with beauty outside upon the wall
Silent ice in the night hung from the trees.

In the gentle night I took a walk with my spirit,
Snow caught my eyes fluttering with little wings,
They try to fly flapping with all their might,
But end up covering the street and soak clothes.

Cold sober response shook the worn knees,
And my tearing teeth broke lamentable silence,
A smitten figure misplace in night ease,
Try to walk outside upon snows frozen ice.

My limbs dug tunnels and tried to hold me tight,
But the ground took my stride to skip and dance,
I walk the path where the street had gone,
For once in my life I felt carried by a spirit.

Along the path set for me with beaten snow,
I started to float and struggle to find a way home,
I should have sunk deep in sleep by now,
Instead, plague with regret; I am out on my own.

I went where footsteps lost their charms,
The softer images in mind losing the fight,
Trying to stay alive swaying with my hips and arms,
The images weren't meant to last through the night.

# Warrant Penitent

Warrant penitent to enter the hidden kingdom
And the full body once young and strong,
Wine and dined serenade with rhapsody
Voices carried along songs to the highest note,
Melodies had turned the world upside down,
Adrenalin laugh out loud force to sing and shout.
By chance and character gold medals are won,
Life was bright and ripe in mind and soul.
Intelligence can never uncover that kingdom,
Behind the veil the atonement was found.
Restore twice as much spirit, body and time,
Hope and love poured grace into our hearts,
Passes inside and enters the secure shrine.
Through the curtain and the moments we find.
The greatest message and the glorious riches,
Gold without value is place by the boatman
Upon The glazed eyes having finally lost control,
They are covered in cold; right and wrong,
To be led by another force into a strange land.

# What might be?

Night rode a long way,
To hide in the dark what might be,
Secrets impossible to find conclusively,
Imagery of light shading the reality.

Mockery from the inside hides the cause,
What might be guilty conscience speaking verbally;
About deeds, and every inept distress,
Tumbling from the head with agony.

Fearful eyes rise in tears to breathe a dismal cry,
What might be taken for granted;
Is often a misconception of reality?
Offering the hope of illusion implanted.

Lusty shadows of night drawing near,
Watched close by dark spirit,
Wandering through the atmosphere,
Expecting the soul to contradict.

Fear tremble beneath the veil of flesh,
Deception covered what might be;
Mercy shielding our secrets in darkness,
Where the intention is to deceive.

# What's In A Kiss?

What's in a kiss that makes me feel better?
Takes us to the place where love is there,
In abundant of unknown things waiting in line
Ready to draw our souls into the corridor of time,
When we are together I become speechless
And each kiss brings our lips closer to touch bliss.
A ray of your smile can brighten up the day
Then my heart searches for reasons to stay
Longer in life to play and hug like we were children
Building bridges in every moment we are given.

To stay together it seems like wishful thinking
With each kiss I will reminisce for a long time,
The bliss in life I will take with me into eternity.
Floating everlasting with the cherish memory.

# When I meet you

Straight from the heart the careless whispers
Race in dreams and a million drop of hopes,
Awake to life and the path of new adventures,
Allowing us to reach into what destiny hides.

When I meet you in that happy state of myself
I will ask if you come and this beautiful planet?
Thorough the clouds that fills yielding breath
You are covered in the belongings of human blanket.

The wind reaches the form of a shape to unveil you
It enter the room where your shadow is standing
Passing through the sunlight and drizzling dew,
And I realize that history is now in the making.

I see the story is dissolving in front of my eyes
And I fall in love with everything that if offers.

# When in darkness

Night without darkness,
Is doing the same as,
Day without sunlight,
Both light and darkness,

Need each other,
To guarantee the cycle of life,
Day and night, summer and winter,
Draw together the years of anxiety and grief.

Along the road of darkness,
Time is paved with experience,
Encounter frustration, hurt and lost,
Love grows with the help of grace.

When in darkness,
Dreams follow life's embrace,
In the fertile seed of rest,
The mind takes healthy shapes.

When in darkness,
Don't look at heights or size,
Treat the imposers as a natural guest,
Listen to the stillness and be wise.

When in darkness,
Be confident in all matter,
The same thing that produce darkness,
Will eventually become clearer.

Hold to unchanging hope,
And rise from obscurity,
To tread the slippery slope,
And find your own security.

# When Love Is Not Enough

When in this land you have given your all,
And not think twice when someone needs forgiven,
Love can cover the hurt every time you fall,
But bruises will be hidden beneath the value of sin.

Even in death love may have its share of grief,
But that will never be enough to comfort the bereaved,
Roaming within the fate of solitude and disbelief,
The search may go on until the heart is relieved.

If love would have been enough to dispel all fear,
You would not be left alone with emotions and regret,
The two protagonists; they find a path more unclear,
And eyes cannot see paradise where there is neglect.

The world we knew was once full and glowing,
But when dreams fled into streams of darker abyss,
Though time may conquer that delta force from within,
Love will never be enough without true happiness.

Paradise was such a beautiful place in our mind,
Exist only when we find time to go there in spirit,
On a trip; in this realm of splendid sublime,
Bliss is given to only those digging deep to find it.

When love is not enough, there is a place to escape,
Found in the wind that floats through the passing air,
Can we dare to go and be where those memories fade?
And fond embrace becomes the only treasure.

# <u>Where Answer Lies</u>

The pledges to bang up freedom
May have no surprises to the guilty,
But destiny offers a sure path to everyone,
To show less is a debt we owe humanity.

Opinion cries out to share with the world,
Where the answer lies in the heart of society,
Isn't it time rulers look out and regain control?
Tackle the root cause of greed or poverty.

We don't want answers to defend people,
As smoke screen from behind glass windows,
To cast a wishful gaze ridiculed with evil,
If trust is taken it will increase our sorrows.

Did our illness come with gentle falling rain?
Rent the cause of discontent battered and brand,
Accruing reasons leading to institute of the insane
To straighten out souls bound for the promise land.

A new principle emerging grants anonymity
And can never be repay with routine excuses,
The affable compensation for poor economy,
Our reward of distress in burnt out promises?

Hoping to carve out something more uniquely
An age tainted by socialism and infirmity,
The past we have managed incoherently,
But the future lies in business and technology.

# Yesterday Today and Tomorrow

Yesterday was here, feeling some pain
Today's gloomy clouds bring a new day,
The misfortunes washed away by the rain,
Tomorrow's raindrops are on the way.

Yesterdays pain, was a beautiful lie
Deranged the senses of our whole frame,
Beguile an ocean of torrid tears to fall,
Self proclaim the inner state in flame.

Today, away from danger hurt and harm
People say the words what others want to hear,
Telling something good in the eye of a storm,
All the while believing what they say is rare.

We change and adopt different moods
When everlasting days goes by eternity
Spirit shapes will drift away with the clouds
Force to stay here others find new destiny.

Tomorrow resurrection comes back rising
Within the veil; love conquers and stand tall
We want to be strong but not too improvising,
Believe to over pain, not just for one but for all.

We paid for yesterday today, with tomorrow
We will find hidden treasures along the way
When our minds find senses in joy and sorrow,
Here to trap us and take our weary soul away.

Guess where they live entirely separate lives
Not just in another world, but now and forever
In many forms vacant space formed paradise,
And over a longer time memories get stronger.

## **You make me feel special**

Under Your spell make me feel special,
Share my doubts, remove all my fears
When you smile I fall under your spell,
You wipe away so many of my tears.

I chase the taste of your lips into the night,
In the moonlight I find bliss securely waiting,
I reach the stars to see the breaking light,
It feels like the sun will never grow dim.

Together we are together connected,
Beyond the prism that friendship has define,
Things we love others may have rejected,
But our love will last for a very long time.

I believe strength can wash away the pain,
You make me forget the sadness for a while
And we can walk together through the rain,
Under your spell love makes me feel special.

Under a spell and make me feel special
Taking the time to say something enchanting,
Then take me to the place of your smile,
You make me feel I was worth something.

# <u>Will you remember me?</u>

Will you remember me?
As time passes away for a little while,
When shadow and fragrance has gone,
You will remember the last smile,
On the day a gentle kissed you gave
Made my soul cried for just a while,
And when you quietly held my hand,
The ribbons of broken flags wave,
Feelings politely tried to understand.
Goodbye to lives intrinsically enjoined,
In the future God had planned.
When we both will go far way,
Into another day of a distinct land,
Remember me when you pray.
I should like to hear your voice,
Once, if you forget what I look like,
Then whisper my name in the air.
And afterwards remember to rejoice,
With memories as though I am right there,
Do not be sorry when broken and contrite
For you was my special choice.
If memory leaves only the silence,
And if I see you once before I go,
With the heritage of thoughts we had.
It is far better that I should know,
You will live happy rather than to be sad.

Sharing life with love

# Title Index

| 40 | ☐ | Contemplation |
| 41 | ☐ | Crumbling Paradise online |
| 42 | ☐ | Dance Recital online |
| 43 | ☐ | Dancing under the Moonlight online |
| 44 | ☐ | Dancing with the stars online |
| 45 | ☐ | Darts of intrigue online |
| 46 | ☐ | Death Passover online |
| 47 | ☐ | Desire |
| 48 | ☐ | Doubt |
| 49 | ☐ | Earth In Upheaval online |
| 50 | ☐ | Empty Promises |

| # | | Title |
| --- | --- | --- |
| 51 | ☐ | England online |
| 52 | ☐ | Experience Of A Lifetime online |
| 53 | ☐ | Fading Away online |
| 54 | ☐ | Fading Spectator online |
| 55 | ☐ | <u>Family memories</u> |
| 56 | ☐ | Farewell |
| 57 | ☐ | Final day of years online |
| 58 | ☐ | Flowers online |
| 59 | ☐ | Fragrant Of My |

Heart online

60 ☐ Freedom Comes

61 ☐ Gathering Dust online

62 ☐ Glimpse of Heaven

63 ☐ God's Assurance

64 ☐ Going where dreams go

65 ☐ Gold within the soul online

66 ☐ Great Is The Son online

67 ☐ Grief

68 ☐ Grow Me Up With Love online

69 ☐ Heaven online

70 ☐ Heaven And Earth

71 ☐ Heavenly Father

72 ☐ Heavenly sunset online

73 ☐ Hope online

74 ☐ Hope Regain

75 ☐ House of Mirrors online

76 ☐ Humanity online

77 ☐ I Am Pressing On online

78 ☐ I don't know why

79 ☐ I know who I am online

80 ☐ I Thought I Could Love You online

81 ☐ I Will Live online

82 ☐ Ice Cream online

83 ☐ I've got you

www.ingramcontent.com/pod-product-compliance
Lightning Source LLC
Chambersburg PA
CBHW071607030726
47593CB00001BA/343